CAREER EXAMINATION SERIES

THIS IS YOUR **PASSBOOK**® FOR ...

CORRECTION OFFICER

NATIONAL LEARNING CORPORATION®
passbooks.com

PASSBOOK® SERIES

THE *PASSBOOK® SERIES* has been created to prepare applicants and candidates for the ultimate academic battlefield – the examination room.

At some time in our lives, each and every one of us may be required to take an examination – for validation, matriculation, admission, qualification, registration, certification, or licensure.

Based on the assumption that every applicant or candidate has met the basic formal educational standards, has taken the required number of courses, and read the necessary texts, the *PASSBOOK® SERIES* furnishes the one special preparation which may assure passing with confidence, instead of failing with insecurity. Examination questions – together with answers – are furnished as the basic vehicle for study so that the mysteries of the examination and its compounding difficulties may be eliminated or diminished by a sure method.

This book is meant to help you pass your examination provided that you qualify and are serious in your objective.

The entire field is reviewed through the huge store of content information which is succinctly presented through a provocative and challenging approach – the question-and-answer method.

A climate of success is established by furnishing the correct answers at the end of each test.

You soon learn to recognize types of questions, forms of questions, and patterns of questioning. You may even begin to anticipate expected outcomes.

You perceive that many questions are repeated or adapted so that you can gain acute insights, which may enable you to score many sure points.

You learn how to confront new questions, or types of questions, and to attack them confidently and work out the correct answers.

You note objectives and emphases, and recognize pitfalls and dangers, so that you may make positive educational adjustments.

Moreover, you are kept fully informed in relation to new concepts, methods, practices, and directions in the field.

You discover that you arre actually taking the examination all the time: you are preparing for the examination by "taking" an examination, not by reading extraneous and/or supererogatory textbooks.

In short, this PASSBOOK®, used directedly, should be an important factor in helping you to pass your test.

CORRECTION OFFICER

DUTIES

Correction Officers, under supervision, maintain security within correctional facilities and are responsible for the custody, control, care, job training and work performance of inmates of detention and sentenced correctional facilities, and perform related work. They supervise inmate meals, visits, recreational programs, and other congregate activities; inspect assigned areas for conditions which threaten safety and security; conduct searches in order to detect contraband; complete forms and reports; maintain appropriate log books; communicate with other area correction officers to exchange pertinent information; issue verbal orders, announcements and explanations to inmates; observe inmates and make recommendations concerning medical and/or psychiatric referrals; safeguard departmental supplies and equipment; escort inmates within and outside of the facility; respond to unusual incidents and disturbances; enforce security procedures in accordance with department guidelines; request medical assistance for inmates when necessary; count and verify the number of inmates present in assigned areas; verify identification of inmates; and supervise inmates.

SCOPE OF THE EXAMINATION

The <u>written test</u> is designed to test for knowledge, skills and/or abilities in such areas as:

1. Observing and recalling facts and information;
2. Applying written information in a correctional services setting;
3. Preparing written material; and
4. Understanding and interpreting written material.

HOW TO TAKE A TEST

I. YOU MUST PASS AN EXAMINATION

A. WHAT EVERY CANDIDATE SHOULD KNOW

Examination applicants often ask us for help in preparing for the written test. What can I study in advance? What kinds of questions will be asked? How will the test be given? How will the papers be graded?

As an applicant for a civil service examination, you may be wondering about some of these things. Our purpose here is to suggest effective methods of advance study and to describe civil service examinations.

Your chances for success on this examination can be increased if you know how to prepare. Those "pre-examination jitters" can be reduced if you know what to expect. You can even experience an adventure in good citizenship if you know why civil service exams are given.

B. WHY ARE CIVIL SERVICE EXAMINATIONS GIVEN?

Civil service examinations are important to you in two ways. As a citizen, you want public jobs filled by employees who know how to do their work. As a job seeker, you want a fair chance to compete for that job on an equal footing with other candidates. The best-known means of accomplishing this two-fold goal is the competitive examination.

Exams are widely publicized throughout the nation. They may be administered for jobs in federal, state, city, municipal, town or village governments or agencies.

Any citizen may apply, with some limitations, such as the age or residence of applicants. Your experience and education may be reviewed to see whether you meet the requirements for the particular examination. When these requirements exist, they are reasonable and applied consistently to all applicants. Thus, a competitive examination may cause you some uneasiness now, but it is your privilege and safeguard.

C. HOW ARE CIVIL SERVICE EXAMS DEVELOPED?

Examinations are carefully written by trained technicians who are specialists in the field known as "psychological measurement," in consultation with recognized authorities in the field of work that the test will cover. These experts recommend the subject matter areas or skills to be tested; only those knowledges or skills important to your success on the job are included. The most reliable books and source materials available are used as references. Together, the experts and technicians judge the difficulty level of the questions.

Test technicians know how to phrase questions so that the problem is clearly stated. Their ethics do not permit "trick" or "catch" questions. Questions may have been tried out on sample groups, or subjected to statistical analysis, to determine their usefulness.

Written tests are often used in combination with performance tests, ratings of training and experience, and oral interviews. All of these measures combine to form the best-known means of finding the right person for the right job.

II. HOW TO PASS THE WRITTEN TEST

A. NATURE OF THE EXAMINATION

To prepare intelligently for civil service examinations, you should know how they differ from school examinations you have taken. In school you were assigned certain definite pages to read or subjects to cover. The examination questions were quite detailed and usually emphasized memory. Civil service exams, on the other hand, try to discover your present ability to perform the duties of a position, plus your potentiality to learn these duties. In other words, a civil service exam attempts to predict how successful you will be. Questions cover such a broad area that they cannot be as minute and detailed as school exam questions.

In the public service similar kinds of work, or positions, are grouped together in one "class." This process is known as *position-classification*. All the positions in a class are paid according to the salary range for that class. One class title covers all of these positions, and they are all tested by the same examination.

B. FOUR BASIC STEPS

1) Study the announcement

How, then, can you know what subjects to study? Our best answer is: "Learn as much as possible about the class of positions for which you've applied." The exam will test the knowledge, skills and abilities needed to do the work.

Your most valuable source of information about the position you want is the official exam announcement. This announcement lists the training and experience qualifications. Check these standards and apply only if you come reasonably close to meeting them.

The brief description of the position in the examination announcement offers some clues to the subjects which will be tested. Think about the job itself. Review the duties in your mind. Can you perform them, or are there some in which you are rusty? Fill in the blank spots in your preparation.

Many jurisdictions preview the written test in the exam announcement by including a section called "Knowledge and Abilities Required," "Scope of the Examination," or some similar heading. Here you will find out specifically what fields will be tested.

2) Review your own background

Once you learn in general what the position is all about, and what you need to know to do the work, ask yourself which subjects you already know fairly well and which need improvement. You may wonder whether to concentrate on improving your strong areas or on building some background in your fields of weakness. When the announcement has specified "some knowledge" or "considerable knowledge," or has used adjectives like "beginning principles of…" or "advanced … methods," you can get a clue as to the number and difficulty of questions to be asked in any given field. More questions, and hence broader coverage, would be included for those subjects which are more important in the work. Now weigh your strengths and weaknesses against the job requirements and prepare accordingly.

3) Determine the level of the position

Another way to tell how intensively you should prepare is to understand the level of the job for which you are applying. Is it the entering level? In other words, is this the position in which beginners in a field of work are hired? Or is it an intermediate or advanced level? Sometimes this is indicated by such words as "Junior" or "Senior" in the class title. Other jurisdictions use Roman numerals to designate the level – Clerk I, Clerk II, for example. The word "Supervisor" sometimes appears in the title. If the level is not indicated by the title, check the description of duties. Will you be working under very close supervision, or will you have responsibility for independent decisions in this work?

4) Choose appropriate study materials

Now that you know the subjects to be examined and the relative amount of each subject to be covered, you can choose suitable study materials. For beginning level jobs, or even advanced ones, if you have a pronounced weakness in some aspect of your training, read a modern, standard textbook in that field. Be sure it is up to date and has general coverage. Such books are normally available at your library, and the librarian will be glad to help you locate one. For entry-level positions, questions of appropriate difficulty are chosen – neither highly advanced questions, nor those too simple. Such questions require careful thought but not advanced training.

If the position for which you are applying is technical or advanced, you will read more advanced, specialized material. If you are already familiar with the basic principles of your field, elementary textbooks would waste your time. Concentrate on advanced textbooks and technical periodicals. Think through the concepts and review difficult problems in your field.

These are all general sources. You can get more ideas on your own initiative, following these leads. For example, training manuals and publications of the government agency which employs workers in your field can be useful, particularly for technical and professional positions. A letter or visit to the government department involved may result in more specific study suggestions, and certainly will provide you with a more definite idea of the exact nature of the position you are seeking.

III. KINDS OF TESTS

Tests are used for purposes other than measuring knowledge and ability to perform specified duties. For some positions, it is equally important to test ability to make adjustments to new situations or to profit from training. In others, basic mental abilities not dependent on information are essential. Questions which test these things may not appear as pertinent to the duties of the position as those which test for knowledge and information. Yet they are often highly important parts of a fair examination. For very general questions, it is almost impossible to help you direct your study efforts. What we can do is to point out some of the more common of these general abilities needed in public service positions and describe some typical questions.

1) General information

Broad, general information has been found useful for predicting job success in some kinds of work. This is tested in a variety of ways, from vocabulary lists to questions about current events. Basic background in some field of work, such as sociology or economics, may be sampled in a group of questions. Often these are principles which have become familiar to most persons through exposure rather than through formal training. It is difficult to advise you how to study for these questions; being alert to the world around you is our best suggestion.

2) Verbal ability

An example of an ability needed in many positions is verbal or language ability. Verbal ability is, in brief, the ability to use and understand words. Vocabulary and grammar tests are typical measures of this ability. Reading comprehension or paragraph interpretation questions are common in many kinds of civil service tests. You are given a paragraph of written material and asked to find its central meaning.

3) Numerical ability

Number skills can be tested by the familiar arithmetic problem, by checking paired lists of numbers to see which are alike and which are different, or by interpreting charts and graphs. In the latter test, a graph may be printed in the test booklet which you are asked to use as the basis for answering questions.

4) Observation

A popular test for law-enforcement positions is the observation test. A picture is shown to you for several minutes, then taken away. Questions about the picture test your ability to observe both details and larger elements.

5) Following directions

In many positions in the public service, the employee must be able to carry out written instructions dependably and accurately. You may be given a chart with several columns, each column listing a variety of information. The questions require you to carry out directions involving the information given in the chart.

6) Skills and aptitudes

Performance tests effectively measure some manual skills and aptitudes. When the skill is one in which you are trained, such as typing or shorthand, you can practice. These tests are often very much like those given in business school or high school courses. For many of the other skills and aptitudes, however, no short-time preparation can be made. Skills and abilities natural to you or that you have developed throughout your lifetime are being tested.

Many of the general questions just described provide all the data needed to answer the questions and ask you to use your reasoning ability to find the answers. Your best preparation for these tests, as well as for tests of facts and ideas, is to be at your physical and mental best. You, no doubt, have your own methods of getting into an exam-taking mood and keeping "in shape." The next section lists some ideas on this subject.

IV. KINDS OF QUESTIONS

Only rarely is the "essay" question, which you answer in narrative form, used in civil service tests. Civil service tests are usually of the short-answer type. Full instructions for answering these questions will be given to you at the examination. But in case this is your first experience with short-answer questions and separate answer sheets, here is what you need to know:

1) Multiple-choice Questions

Most popular of the short-answer questions is the "multiple choice" or "best answer" question. It can be used, for example, to test for factual knowledge, ability to solve problems or judgment in meeting situations found at work.

A multiple-choice question is normally one of three types—

- It can begin with an incomplete statement followed by several possible endings. You are to find the one ending which *best* completes the statement, although some of the others may not be entirely wrong.
- It can also be a complete statement in the form of a question which is answered by choosing one of the statements listed.
- It can be in the form of a problem – again you select the best answer.

Here is an example of a multiple-choice question with a discussion which should give you some clues as to the method for choosing the right answer:

When an employee has a complaint about his assignment, the action which will *best* help him overcome his difficulty is to
A. discuss his difficulty with his coworkers
B. take the problem to the head of the organization
C. take the problem to the person who gave him the assignment
D. say nothing to anyone about his complaint

In answering this question, you should study each of the choices to find which is best. Consider choice "A" – Certainly an employee may discuss his complaint with fellow employees, but no change or improvement can result, and the complaint remains unresolved. Choice "B" is a poor choice since the head of the organization probably does not know what assignment you have been given, and taking your problem to him is known as "going over the head" of the supervisor. The supervisor, or person who made the assignment, is the person who can clarify it or correct any injustice. Choice "C" is, therefore, correct. To say nothing, as in choice "D," is unwise. Supervisors have and interest in knowing the problems employees are facing, and the employee is seeking a solution to his problem.

2) True/False Questions

The "true/false" or "right/wrong" form of question is sometimes used. Here a complete statement is given. Your job is to decide whether the statement is right or wrong.

SAMPLE: A roaming cell-phone call to a nearby city costs less than a non-roaming call to a distant city.

This statement is wrong, or false, since roaming calls are more expensive.
This is not a complete list of all possible question forms, although most of the others are variations of these common types. You will always get complete directions for

answering questions. Be sure you understand *how* to mark your answers – ask questions until you do.

V. RECORDING YOUR ANSWERS

Computer terminals are used more and more today for many different kinds of exams.

For an examination with very few applicants, you may be told to record your answers in the test booklet itself. Separate answer sheets are much more common. If this separate answer sheet is to be scored by machine – and this is often the case – it is highly important that you mark your answers correctly in order to get credit.

An electronic scoring machine is often used in civil service offices because of the speed with which papers can be scored. Machine-scored answer sheets must be marked with a pencil, which will be given to you. This pencil has a high graphite content which responds to the electronic scoring machine. As a matter of fact, stray dots may register as answers, so do not let your pencil rest on the answer sheet while you are pondering the correct answer. Also, if your pencil lead breaks or is otherwise defective, ask for another.

Since the answer sheet will be dropped in a slot in the scoring machine, be careful not to bend the corners or get the paper crumpled.

The answer sheet normally has five vertical columns of numbers, with 30 numbers to a column. These numbers correspond to the question numbers in your test booklet. After each number, going across the page are four or five pairs of dotted lines. These short dotted lines have small letters or numbers above them. The first two pairs may also have a "T" or "F" above the letters. This indicates that the first two pairs only are to be used if the questions are of the true-false type. If the questions are multiple choice, disregard the "T" and "F" and pay attention only to the small letters or numbers.

Answer your questions in the manner of the sample that follows:

32. The largest city in the United States is
    A. Washington, D.C.
    B. New York City
    C. Chicago
    D. Detroit
    E. San Francisco

1) Choose the answer you think is best. (New York City is the largest, so "B" is correct.)
2) Find the row of dotted lines numbered the same as the question you are answering. (Find row number 32)
3) Find the pair of dotted lines corresponding to the answer. (Find the pair of lines under the mark "B.")
4) Make a solid black mark between the dotted lines.

VI. BEFORE THE TEST

Common sense will help you find procedures to follow to get ready for an examination. Too many of us, however, overlook these sensible measures. Indeed, nervousness and fatigue have been found to be the most serious reasons why applicants fail to do their best on civil service tests. Here is a list of reminders:

- Begin your preparation early – Don't wait until the last minute to go scurrying around for books and materials or to find out what the position is all about.
- Prepare continuously – An hour a night for a week is better than an all-night cram session. This has been definitely established. What is more, a night a week for a month will return better dividends than crowding your study into a shorter period of time.
- Locate the place of the exam – You have been sent a notice telling you when and where to report for the examination. If the location is in a different town or otherwise unfamiliar to you, it would be well to inquire the best route and learn something about the building.
- Relax the night before the test – Allow your mind to rest. Do not study at all that night. Plan some mild recreation or diversion; then go to bed early and get a good night's sleep.
- Get up early enough to make a leisurely trip to the place for the test – This way unforeseen events, traffic snarls, unfamiliar buildings, etc. will not upset you.
- Dress comfortably – A written test is not a fashion show. You will be known by number and not by name, so wear something comfortable.
- Leave excess paraphernalia at home – Shopping bags and odd bundles will get in your way. You need bring only the items mentioned in the official notice you received; usually everything you need is provided. Do not bring reference books to the exam. They will only confuse those last minutes and be taken away from you when in the test room.
- Arrive somewhat ahead of time – If because of transportation schedules you must get there very early, bring a newspaper or magazine to take your mind off yourself while waiting.
- Locate the examination room – When you have found the proper room, you will be directed to the seat or part of the room where you will sit. Sometimes you are given a sheet of instructions to read while you are waiting. Do not fill out any forms until you are told to do so; just read them and be prepared.
- Relax and prepare to listen to the instructions
- If you have any physical problem that may keep you from doing your best, be sure to tell the test administrator. If you are sick or in poor health, you really cannot do your best on the exam. You can come back and take the test some other time.

VII. AT THE TEST

The day of the test is here and you have the test booklet in your hand. The temptation to get going is very strong. Caution! There is more to success than knowing the right answers. You must know how to identify your papers and understand variations in the type of short-answer question used in this particular examination. Follow these suggestions for maximum results from your efforts:

1) Cooperate with the monitor

The test administrator has a duty to create a situation in which you can be as much at ease as possible. He will give instructions, tell you when to begin, check to see that you are marking your answer sheet correctly, and so on. He is not there to guard you, although he will see that your competitors do not take unfair advantage. He wants to help you do your best.

2) Listen to all instructions

Don't jump the gun! Wait until you understand all directions. In most civil service tests you get more time than you need to answer the questions. So don't be in a hurry. Read each word of instructions until you clearly understand the meaning. Study the examples, listen to all announcements and follow directions. Ask questions if you do not understand what to do.

3) Identify your papers

Civil service exams are usually identified by number only. You will be assigned a number; you must not put your name on your test papers. Be sure to copy your number correctly. Since more than one exam may be given, copy your exact examination title.

4) Plan your time

Unless you are told that a test is a "speed" or "rate of work" test, speed itself is usually not important. Time enough to answer all the questions will be provided, but this does not mean that you have all day. An overall time limit has been set. Divide the total time (in minutes) by the number of questions to determine the approximate time you have for each question.

5) Do not linger over difficult questions

If you come across a difficult question, mark it with a paper clip (useful to have along) and come back to it when you have been through the booklet. One caution if you do this – be sure to skip a number on your answer sheet as well. Check often to be sure that you have not lost your place and that you are marking in the row numbered the same as the question you are answering.

6) Read the questions

Be sure you know what the question asks! Many capable people are unsuccessful because they failed to *read* the questions correctly.

7) Answer all questions

Unless you have been instructed that a penalty will be deducted for incorrect answers, it is better to guess than to omit a question.

8) Speed tests

It is often better NOT to guess on speed tests. It has been found that on timed tests people are tempted to spend the last few seconds before time is called in marking answers at random – without even reading them – in the hope of picking up a few extra points. To discourage this practice, the instructions may warn you that your score will be "corrected" for guessing. That is, a penalty will be applied. The incorrect answers will be deducted from the correct ones, or some other penalty formula will be used.

9) Review your answers

If you finish before time is called, go back to the questions you guessed or omitted to give them further thought. Review other answers if you have time.

10) Return your test materials

If you are ready to leave before others have finished or time is called, take ALL your materials to the monitor and leave quietly. Never take any test material with you. The monitor can discover whose papers are not complete, and taking a test booklet may be grounds for disqualification.

VIII. EXAMINATION TECHNIQUES

1) Read the general instructions carefully. These are usually printed on the first page of the exam booklet. As a rule, these instructions refer to the timing of the examination; the fact that you should not start work until the signal and must stop work at a signal, etc. If there are any *special* instructions, such as a choice of questions to be answered, make sure that you note this instruction carefully.

2) When you are ready to start work on the examination, that is as soon as the signal has been given, read the instructions to each question booklet, underline any key words or phrases, such as *least, best, outline, describe* and the like. In this way you will tend to answer as requested rather than discover on reviewing your paper that you *listed without describing*, that you selected the *worst* choice rather than the *best* choice, etc.

3) If the examination is of the objective or multiple-choice type – that is, each question will also give a series of possible answers: A, B, C or D, and you are called upon to select the best answer and write the letter next to that answer on your answer paper – it is advisable to start answering each question in turn. There may be anywhere from 50 to 100 such questions in the three or four hours allotted and you can see how much time would be taken if you read through all the questions before beginning to answer any. Furthermore, if you come across a question or group of questions which you know would be difficult to answer, it would undoubtedly affect your handling of all the other questions.

4) If the examination is of the essay type and contains but a few questions, it is a moot point as to whether you should read all the questions before starting to answer any one. Of course, if you are given a choice – say five out of seven and the like – then it is essential to read all the questions so you can eliminate the two that are most difficult. If, however, you are asked to answer all the questions, there may be danger in trying to answer the easiest one first because you may find that you will spend too much time on it. The best technique is to answer the first question, then proceed to the second, etc.

5) Time your answers. Before the exam begins, write down the time it started, then add the time allowed for the examination and write down the time it must be completed, then divide the time available somewhat as follows:

- If 3-1/2 hours are allowed, that would be 210 minutes. If you have 80 objective-type questions, that would be an average of 2-1/2 minutes per question. Allow yourself no more than 2 minutes per question, or a total of 160 minutes, which will permit about 50 minutes to review.
- If for the time allotment of 210 minutes there are 7 essay questions to answer, that would average about 30 minutes a question. Give yourself only 25 minutes per question so that you have about 35 minutes to review.

6) The most important instruction is to *read each question* and make sure you know what is wanted. The second most important instruction is to *time yourself properly* so that you answer every question. The third most important instruction is to *answer every question*. Guess if you have to but include something for each question. Remember that you will receive no credit for a blank and will probably receive some credit if you write something in answer to an essay question. If you guess a letter – say "B" for a multiple-choice question – you may have guessed right. If you leave a blank as an answer to a multiple-choice question, the examiners may respect your feelings but it will not add a point to your score. Some exams may penalize you for wrong answers, so in such cases *only*, you may not want to guess unless you have some basis for your answer.

7) Suggestions
   a. Objective-type questions
      1. Examine the question booklet for proper sequence of pages and questions
      2. Read all instructions carefully
      3. Skip any question which seems too difficult; return to it after all other questions have been answered
      4. Apportion your time properly; do not spend too much time on any single question or group of questions
      5. Note and underline key words – *all, most, fewest, least, best, worst, same, opposite,* etc.
      6. Pay particular attention to negatives
      7. Note unusual option, e.g., unduly long, short, complex, different or similar in content to the body of the question
      8. Observe the use of "hedging" words – *probably, may, most likely,* etc.
      9. Make sure that your answer is put next to the same number as the question
      10. Do not second-guess unless you have good reason to believe the second answer is definitely more correct
      11. Cross out original answer if you decide another answer is more accurate; do not erase until you are ready to hand your paper in
      12. Answer all questions; guess unless instructed otherwise
      13. Leave time for review

   b. Essay questions
      1. Read each question carefully
      2. Determine exactly what is wanted. Underline key words or phrases.
      3. Decide on outline or paragraph answer

4. Include many different points and elements unless asked to develop any one or two points or elements
5. Show impartiality by giving pros and cons unless directed to select one side only
6. Make and write down any assumptions you find necessary to answer the questions
7. Watch your English, grammar, punctuation and choice of words
8. Time your answers; don't crowd material

8) Answering the essay question

Most essay questions can be answered by framing the specific response around several key words or ideas. Here are a few such key words or ideas:

M's: manpower, materials, methods, money, management
P's: purpose, program, policy, plan, procedure, practice, problems, pitfalls, personnel, public relations
a. Six basic steps in handling problems:
1. Preliminary plan and background development
2. Collect information, data and facts
3. Analyze and interpret information, data and facts
4. Analyze and develop solutions as well as make recommendations
5. Prepare report and sell recommendations
6. Install recommendations and follow up effectiveness

b. Pitfalls to avoid
1. *Taking things for granted* – A statement of the situation does not necessarily imply that each of the elements is necessarily true; for example, a complaint may be invalid and biased so that all that can be taken for granted is that a complaint has been registered
2. *Considering only one side of a situation* – Wherever possible, indicate several alternatives and then point out the reasons you selected the best one
3. *Failing to indicate follow up* – Whenever your answer indicates action on your part, make certain that you will take proper follow-up action to see how successful your recommendations, procedures or actions turn out to be
4. *Taking too long in answering any single question* – Remember to time your answers properly

IX. AFTER THE TEST

Scoring procedures differ in detail among civil service jurisdictions although the general principles are the same. Whether the papers are hand-scored or graded by machine we have described, they are nearly always graded by number. That is, the person who marks the paper knows only the number – never the name – of the applicant. Not until all the papers have been graded will they be matched with names. If other tests, such as training and experience or oral interview ratings have been given, scores will be combined. Different parts of the examination usually have different weights. For example, the written test might count 60 percent of the final grade, and a rating of training and experience 40 percent. In many jurisdictions, veterans will have a certain number of points added to their grades.

After the final grade has been determined, the names are placed in grade order and an eligible list is established. There are various methods for resolving ties between those who get the same final grade – probably the most common is to place first the name of the person whose application was received first. Job offers are made from the eligible list in the order the names appear on it. You will be notified of your grade and your rank as soon as all these computations have been made. This will be done as rapidly as possible.

People who are found to meet the requirements in the announcement are called "eligibles." Their names are put on a list of eligible candidates. An eligible's chances of getting a job depend on how high he stands on this list and how fast agencies are filling jobs from the list.

When a job is to be filled from a list of eligibles, the agency asks for the names of people on the list of eligibles for that job. When the civil service commission receives this request, it sends to the agency the names of the three people highest on this list. Or, if the job to be filled has specialized requirements, the office sends the agency the names of the top three persons who meet these requirements from the general list.

The appointing officer makes a choice from among the three people whose names were sent to him. If the selected person accepts the appointment, the names of the others are put back on the list to be considered for future openings.

That is the rule in hiring from all kinds of eligible lists, whether they are for typist, carpenter, chemist, or something else. For every vacancy, the appointing officer has his choice of any one of the top three eligibles on the list. This explains why the person whose name is on top of the list sometimes does not get an appointment when some of the persons lower on the list do. If the appointing officer chooses the second or third eligible, the No. 1 eligible does not get a job at once, but stays on the list until he is appointed or the list is terminated.

X. HOW TO PASS THE INTERVIEW TEST

The examination for which you applied requires an oral interview test. You have already taken the written test and you are now being called for the interview test – the final part of the formal examination.

You may think that it is not possible to prepare for an interview test and that there are no procedures to follow during an interview. Our purpose is to point out some things you can do in advance that will help you and some good rules to follow and pitfalls to avoid while you are being interviewed.

What is an interview supposed to test?
The written examination is designed to test the technical knowledge and competence of the candidate; the oral is designed to evaluate intangible qualities, not readily measured otherwise, and to establish a list showing the relative fitness of each candidate – as measured against his competitors – for the position sought. Scoring is not on the basis of "right" and "wrong," but on a sliding scale of values ranging from "not passable" to "outstanding." As a matter of fact, it is possible to achieve a relatively low score without a single "incorrect" answer because of evident weakness in the qualities being measured.

Occasionally, an examination may consist entirely of an oral test – either an individual or a group oral. In such cases, information is sought concerning the technical knowledges and abilities of the candidate, since there has been no written examination for this purpose. More commonly, however, an oral test is used to supplement a written examination.

Who conducts interviews?

The composition of oral boards varies among different jurisdictions. In nearly all, a representative of the personnel department serves as chairman. One of the members of the board may be a representative of the department in which the candidate would work. In some cases, "outside experts" are used, and, frequently, a businessman or some other representative of the general public is asked to serve. Labor and management or other special groups may be represented. The aim is to secure the services of experts in the appropriate field.

However the board is composed, it is a good idea (and not at all improper or unethical) to ascertain in advance of the interview who the members are and what groups they represent. When you are introduced to them, you will have some idea of their backgrounds and interests, and at least you will not stutter and stammer over their names.

What should be done before the interview?

While knowledge about the board members is useful and takes some of the surprise element out of the interview, there is other preparation which is more substantive. It *is* possible to prepare for an oral interview – in several ways:

1) Keep a copy of your application and review it carefully before the interview

This may be the only document before the oral board, and the starting point of the interview. Know what education and experience you have listed there, and the sequence and dates of all of it. Sometimes the board will ask you to review the highlights of your experience for them; you should not have to hem and haw doing it.

2) Study the class specification and the examination announcement

Usually, the oral board has one or both of these to guide them. The qualities, characteristics or knowledges required by the position sought are stated in these documents. They offer valuable clues as to the nature of the oral interview. For example, if the job involves supervisory responsibilities, the announcement will usually indicate that knowledge of modern supervisory methods and the qualifications of the candidate as a supervisor will be tested. If so, you can expect such questions, frequently in the form of a hypothetical situation which you are expected to solve. NEVER go into an oral without knowledge of the duties and responsibilities of the job you seek.

3) Think through each qualification required

Try to visualize the kind of questions you would ask if you were a board member. How well could you answer them? Try especially to appraise your own knowledge and background in each area, *measured against the job sought*, and identify any areas in which you are weak. Be critical and realistic – do not flatter yourself.

4) Do some general reading in areas in which you feel you may be weak

For example, if the job involves supervision and your past experience has NOT, some general reading in supervisory methods and practices, particularly in the field of human relations, might be useful. Do NOT study agency procedures or detailed manuals. The oral board will be testing your understanding and capacity, not your memory.

5) Get a good night's sleep and watch your general health and mental attitude

You will want a clear head at the interview. Take care of a cold or any other minor ailment, and of course, no hangovers.

What should be done on the day of the interview?

Now comes the day of the interview itself. Give yourself plenty of time to get there. Plan to arrive somewhat ahead of the scheduled time, particularly if your appointment is in the fore part of the day. If a previous candidate fails to appear, the board might be ready for you a bit early. By early afternoon an oral board is almost invariably behind schedule if there are many candidates, and you may have to wait. Take along a book or magazine to read, or your application to review, but leave any extraneous material in the waiting room when you go in for your interview. In any event, relax and compose yourself.

The matter of dress is important. The board is forming impressions about you – from your experience, your manners, your attitude, and your appearance. Give your personal appearance careful attention. Dress your best, but not your flashiest. Choose conservative, appropriate clothing, and be sure it is immaculate. This is a business interview, and your appearance should indicate that you regard it as such. Besides, being well groomed and properly dressed will help boost your confidence.

Sooner or later, someone will call your name and escort you into the interview room. *This is it.* From here on you are on your own. It is too late for any more preparation. But remember, you asked for this opportunity to prove your fitness, and you are here because your request was granted.

What happens when you go in?

The usual sequence of events will be as follows: The clerk (who is often the board stenographer) will introduce you to the chairman of the oral board, who will introduce you to the other members of the board. Acknowledge the introductions before you sit down. Do not be surprised if you find a microphone facing you or a stenotypist sitting by. Oral interviews are usually recorded in the event of an appeal or other review.

Usually the chairman of the board will open the interview by reviewing the highlights of your education and work experience from your application – primarily for the benefit of the other members of the board, as well as to get the material into the record. Do not interrupt or comment unless there is an error or significant misinterpretation; if that is the case, do not hesitate. But do not quibble about insignificant matters. Also, he will usually ask you some question about your education, experience or your present job – partly to get you to start talking and to establish the interviewing "rapport." He may start the actual questioning, or turn it over to one of the other members. Frequently, each member undertakes the questioning on a particular area, one in which he is perhaps most competent, so you can expect each member to participate in the examination. Because time is limited, you may also expect some rather abrupt switches in the direction the questioning takes, so do not be upset by it. Normally, a board member will not pursue a single line of questioning unless he discovers a particular strength or weakness.

After each member has participated, the chairman will usually ask whether any member has any further questions, then will ask you if you have anything you wish to add. Unless you are expecting this question, it may floor you. Worse, it may start you off on an extended, extemporaneous speech. The board is not usually seeking more information. The question is principally to offer you a last opportunity to present further qualifications or to indicate that you have nothing to add. So, if you feel that a significant qualification or characteristic has been overlooked, it is proper to point it out in a sentence or so. Do not compliment the board on the thoroughness of their examination – they have been sketchy, and you know it. If you wish, merely say, "No thank you, I have nothing further to add." This is a point where you can "talk yourself out" of a good impression or fail to present an important bit of information. Remember, *you close the interview yourself.*

The chairman will then say, "That is all, Mr. _____, thank you." Do not be startled; the interview is over, and quicker than you think. Thank him, gather your belongings and take your leave. Save your sigh of relief for the other side of the door.

How to put your best foot forward

Throughout this entire process, you may feel that the board individually and collectively is trying to pierce your defenses, seek out your hidden weaknesses and embarrass and confuse you. Actually, this is not true. They are obliged to make an appraisal of your qualifications for the job you are seeking, and they want to see you in your best light. Remember, they must interview all candidates and a non-cooperative candidate may become a failure in spite of their best efforts to bring out his qualifications. Here are 15 suggestions that will help you:

1) Be natural – Keep your attitude confident, not cocky

If you are not confident that you can do the job, do not expect the board to be. Do not apologize for your weaknesses, try to bring out your strong points. The board is interested in a positive, not negative, presentation. Cockiness will antagonize any board member and make him wonder if you are covering up a weakness by a false show of strength.

2) Get comfortable, but don't lounge or sprawl

Sit erectly but not stiffly. A careless posture may lead the board to conclude that you are careless in other things, or at least that you are not impressed by the importance of the occasion. Either conclusion is natural, even if incorrect. Do not fuss with your clothing, a pencil or an ashtray. Your hands may occasionally be useful to emphasize a point; do not let them become a point of distraction.

3) Do not wisecrack or make small talk

This is a serious situation, and your attitude should show that you consider it as such. Further, the time of the board is limited – they do not want to waste it, and neither should you.

4) Do not exaggerate your experience or abilities

In the first place, from information in the application or other interviews and sources, the board may know more about you than you think. Secondly, you probably will not get away with it. An experienced board is rather adept at spotting such a situation, so do not take the chance.

5) If you know a board member, do not make a point of it, yet do not hide it

Certainly you are not fooling him, and probably not the other members of the board. Do not try to take advantage of your acquaintanceship – it will probably do you little good.

6) Do not dominate the interview

Let the board do that. They will give you the clues – do not assume that you have to do all the talking. Realize that the board has a number of questions to ask you, and do not try to take up all the interview time by showing off your extensive knowledge of the answer to the first one.

7) Be attentive

You only have 20 minutes or so, and you should keep your attention at its sharpest throughout. When a member is addressing a problem or question to you, give him your undivided attention. Address your reply principally to him, but do not exclude the other board members.

8) Do not interrupt

A board member may be stating a problem for you to analyze. He will ask you a question when the time comes. Let him state the problem, and wait for the question.

9) Make sure you understand the question

Do not try to answer until you are sure what the question is. If it is not clear, restate it in your own words or ask the board member to clarify it for you. However, do not haggle about minor elements.

10) Reply promptly but not hastily

A common entry on oral board rating sheets is "candidate responded readily," or "candidate hesitated in replies." Respond as promptly and quickly as you can, but do not jump to a hasty, ill-considered answer.

11) Do not be peremptory in your answers

A brief answer is proper – but do not fire your answer back. That is a losing game from your point of view. The board member can probably ask questions much faster than you can answer them.

12) Do not try to create the answer you think the board member wants

He is interested in what kind of mind you have and how it works – not in playing games. Furthermore, he can usually spot this practice and will actually grade you down on it.

13) Do not switch sides in your reply merely to agree with a board member

Frequently, a member will take a contrary position merely to draw you out and to see if you are willing and able to defend your point of view. Do not start a debate, yet do not surrender a good position. If a position is worth taking, it is worth defending.

14) Do not be afraid to admit an error in judgment if you are shown to be wrong

The board knows that you are forced to reply without any opportunity for careful consideration. Your answer may be demonstrably wrong. If so, admit it and get on with the interview.

15) Do not dwell at length on your present job

The opening question may relate to your present assignment. Answer the question but do not go into an extended discussion. You are being examined for a *new* job, not your present one. As a matter of fact, try to phrase ALL your answers in terms of the job for which you are being examined.

Basis of Rating

Probably you will forget most of these "do's" and "don'ts" when you walk into the oral interview room. Even remembering them all will not ensure you a passing grade. Perhaps you did not have the qualifications in the first place. But remembering them will help you to put your best foot forward, without treading on the toes of the board members.

Rumor and popular opinion to the contrary notwithstanding, an oral board wants you to make the best appearance possible. They know you are under pressure – but they also want to see how you respond to it as a guide to what your reaction would be under the pressures of the job you seek. They will be influenced by the degree of poise you display, the personal traits you show and the manner in which you respond.

ABOUT THIS BOOK

This book contains tests divided into Examination Sections. Go through each test, answering every question in the margin. At the end of each test look at the answer key and check your answers. On the ones you got wrong, look at the right answer choice and learn. Do not fill in the answers first. Do not memorize the questions and answers, but understand the answer and principles involved. On your test, the questions will likely be different from the samples. Questions are changed and new ones added. If you understand these past questions you should have success with any changes that arise. Tests may consist of several types of questions. We have additional books on each subject should more study be advisable or necessary for you. Finally, the more you study, the better prepared you will be. This book is intended to be the last thing you study before you walk into the examination room. Prior study of relevant texts is also recommended. NLC publishes some of these in our Fundamental Series. Knowledge and good sense are important factors in passing your exam. Good luck also helps. So now study this Passbook, absorb the material contained within and take that knowledge into the examination. Then do your best to pass that exam.

———

EXAMINATION SECTION

EXAMINATION SECTION
TEST 1

DIRECTIONS: Each question or incomplete statement is followed by several suggested answers or completions. Select the one that BEST answers the question or completes the statement. *PRINT THE LETTER OF THE CORRECT ANSWER IN THE SPACE AT THE RIGHT.*

1. Physical and mental health are essential to the officer. According to this statement, the officer MUST be

    A. as wise as he is strong
    B. smarter than most people
    C. sound in mind and body
    D. stronger than the average criminal

1._____

2. Teamwork is the basis of successful law enforcement. The factor stressed by this statement is

    A. cooperation
    C. initiative
    B. determination
    D. pride

2._____

3. Legal procedure is a means, not an end. Its function is merely to accomplish the enforcement of legal rights. A litigant has no vested interest in the observance of the rules of procedure as such. All that he should be entitled to demand is that he be given an opportunity for a fair and impartial trial of his case. He should not be permitted to invoke the aid of technical rules merely to embarrass his adversary.
    According to this paragraph, it is MOST correct to state that

    A. observance of the rules of procedure guarantees a fair trial
    B. embarrassment of an adversary through technical rules does not make a fair trial
    C. a litigant is not interested in the observance of rules of procedure
    D. technical rules must not be used in a trial

3._____

4. One theory states that all criminal behavior is taught by a process of communication within small intimate groups. An individual engages in criminal behavior if the number of criminal patterns which he has acquired exceed the number of non-criminal patterns. This statement indicates that criminal behavior is

    A. learned
    C. hereditary
    B. instinctive
    D. reprehensible

4._____

5. The law enforcement staff of today requires training and mental qualities of a high order. The poorly or partially prepared staff member lowers the standard of work, retards his own earning power, and fails in a career meant to provide a livelihood and social improvement.
    According to this statement,

    A. an inefficient member of a law enforcement staff will still earn a good livelihood
    B. law enforcement officers move in good social circles
    C. many people fail in law enforcement careers
    D. persons of training and ability are essential to a law enforcement staff

5._____

6. In any state, no crime can occur unless there is a written law forbidding the act or the omission in question; and even though an act may not be exactly in harmony with public policy, such act is not a crime unless it is expressly forbidden by legislative enactment. According to the above statement,

    A. a crime is committed with reference to a particular law
    B. acts not in harmony with public policy should be forbidden by law
    C. non-criminal activity will promote public welfare
    D. legislative enactments frequently forbid actions in harmony with public policy

6.___

7. The unrestricted sale of firearms is one of the main causes of our shameful crime record. According to this statement, one of the causes of our crime record is

    A. development of firepower
    B. ease of securing weapons
    C. increased skill in using guns
    D. scientific perfection of firearms

7.___

8. Every person must be informed of the reason for his arrest unless he is arrested in the actual commission of a crime. Sufficient force to effect the arrest may be used, but the courts frown on brutal methods. According to this statement, a person does not have to be informed of the reason for his arrest if

    A. brutal force was not used in effecting it
    B. the courts will later turn the defendant loose
    C. the person arrested knows force will be used if necessary
    D. the reason for it is clearly evident from the circumstances

8.___

9. An important duty of an officer is to keep order in the court.
On the basis of this statement, it is probably true that

    A. it is more important for an officer to be strong than it is for him to be smart
    B. people involved in court trials are noisy if not kept in check
    C. not every duty of an officer is important
    D. the maintenance of order is important for the proper conduct of court business

9.___

10. Ideally, a correctional system should include several types of institutions to provide different degrees of custody.
On the basis of this statement, one could MOST reasonably say that

    A. as the number of institutions in a correctional system increases, the efficiency of the system increases
    B. the difference in degree of custody for the inmate depends on the types of institutions in a correctional system
    C. the greater the variety of institutions, the stricter the degree of custody that can be maintained
    D. the same type of correctional institution is not desirable for the custody of all prisoners

10.___

11. The enforced idleness of a large percentage of adult men and women in our prisons is one of the direct causes of the tensions which burst forth in riot and disorder.
On the basis of this statement, a good reason why inmates should perform daily work of some kind is that

11.___

A. better morale and discipline can be maintained when inmates are kept busy
B. daily work is an effective way of punishing inmates for the crimes they have committed
C. law-abiding citizens must work; therefore, labor should also be required of inmates
D. products of inmates' labor will, in part, pay the cost of their maintenance

12. With industry invading rural areas, the use of the automobile, and the speed of modern   12._____
communications and transportation, the problems of neglect and delinquency are no
longer peculiar to cities but an established feature of everyday life.
This statement implies MOST directly that

    A. delinquents are moving from cities to rural areas
    B. delinquency and neglect are found in rural areas
    C. delinquency is not as much of a problem in rural areas as in cities
    D. rural areas now surpass cities in industry

13. Young men from minority groups, if unable to find employment, become discouraged and   13._____
hopeless because of their economic position and may finally resort to any means of sup-
plying their wants.
The MOST reasonable of the following conclusions that may be drawn from this statement only is that

    A. discouragement sometimes leads to crime
    B. in general, young men from minority groups are criminals
    C. unemployment turns young men from crime
    D. young men from minority groups are seldom employed

14. To prevent crime, we must deal with the possible criminal long before he reaches the   14._____
prison. Our aim should be not merely to reform the law breakers but to strike at the roots
of crime: neglectful parents, bad companions, unsatisfactory homes, selfishness, disregard for the rights of others, and bad social conditions.
The above statement recommends

    A. abolition of prisons   B. better reformatories
    C. compulsory education   D. general social reform

15. There is evidence which shows that comic books which glorify the criminal and criminal   15._____
acts have a distinct influence in producing young criminals.
According to this statement,

    A. comic books affect the development of criminal careers
    B. comic books specialize in reporting criminal acts
    C. young criminals read comic books exclusively
    D. young criminals should not be permitted to read comic books

16. Suppose a study shows that juvenile delinquents are equal in intelligence but three   16._____
school grades behind juvenile non-delinquents.
On the basis of this information only, it is MOST reasonable to say that

    A. a delinquent usually progresses to the educational limit set by his intelligence
    B. educational achievement depends on intelligence only
    C. educational achievement is closely associated with delinquency
    D. lack of intelligence is closely associated with delinquency

17. There is no proof today that the experience of a prison sentence makes a better citizen of an adult. On the contrary, there seems some evidence that the experience is an unwholesome one that frequently confirms the criminality of the inmate.
From the above paragraph only, it may be BEST concluded that

    A. prison sentences tend to punish rather than rehabilitate
    B. all criminals should be given prison sentences
    C. we should abandon our penal institutions
    D. penal institutions are effective in rehabilitating criminals

17.___

18. Some courts are referred to as *criminal* courts while others are known as *civil* courts. This distinction in name is MOST probably based on the

    A. historical origin of the court
    B. link between the court and the police
    C. manner in which the judges are chosen
    D. type of cases tried there

18.___

19. Many children who are exposed to contacts and experiences of a delinquent nature become educated and trained in crime in the course of participating in the daily life of the neighborhood.
From this statement only, we may reasonably conclude that

    A. delinquency passes from parent to child
    B. neighborhood influences are usually bad
    C. schools are training grounds for delinquents
    D. none of the above conclusions is reasonable

19.___

20. Old age insurance, for whose benefits a quarter of a million city employees may elect to become eligible, is one feature of the Social Security Act that is wholly administered by the Federal government.
On the basis of this paragraph only, it may MOST reasonably be inferred that

    A. a quarter of a million city employees are drawing old age insurance
    B. a quarter of a million city employees have elected to become eligible for old age insurance
    C. the city has no part in administering Social Security old age insurance
    D. only the Federal government administers the Social Security Act

20.___

21. An officer's revolver is a defensive, and not offensive, weapon.
On the basis of this statement only, an officer should BEST draw his revolver to

    A. fire at an unarmed burglar
    B. force a suspect to confess
    C. frighten a juvenile delinquent
    D. protect his own life

21.___

22. Prevention of crime is of greater value to the community than the punishment of crime.
If this statement is accepted as true, GREATEST emphasis should be placed on

    A. malingering   B. medication
    C. imprisonment   D. rehabilitation

22.___

23. The criminal is rarely or never reformed. Acceptance of this statement as true would mean that GREATEST emphasis should be placed on   23._____

    A. imprisonment   B. parole
    C. probation   D. malingering

24. The MOST accurate of the following statements about persons convicted of crimes is that   24._____

    A. their criminal behavior is almost invariably the result of low intelligence
    B. they are almost invariably legally insane
    C. they are more likely to come from underprivileged groups than from other groups
    D. they have certain facial characteristics which distinguish them from non-criminals

25. Suppose a study shows that the I.Q. (Intelligence Quotient) of prison inmates is 95 as opposed to an I.Q. of 100 for a numerically equivalent civilian group.
A claim, on the basis of this study, that criminals have a lower I.Q. than non-criminals would be   25._____

    A. *improper;* prison inmates are criminals who have been caught
    B. *proper;* the study was numerically well done
    C. *improper;* the sample was inadequate
    D. *proper;* even misdemeanors are sometimes penalized by prison sentences

Questions 26-45.

DIRECTIONS: In answering Questions 26 through 45, select the letter of the word or expression that MOST NEARLY expresses the meaning of the capitalized word in the group.

26. ABDUCT   26._____

    A. lead   B. kidnap   C. sudden   D. worthless

27. BIAS   27._____

    A. ability   B. envy   C. prejudice   D. privilege

28. COERCE   28._____

    A. cancel   B. force   C. rescind   D. rugged

29. CONDONE   29._____

    A. combine   B. pardon   C. revive   D. spice

30. CONSISTENCY   30._____

    A. bravery   B. readiness   C. strain   D. uniformity

31. CREDENCE   31._____

    A. belief   B. devotion   C. resemblance   D. tempo

32. CURRENT   32._____

    A. backward   B. brave   C. prevailing   D. wary

33. CUSTODY

    A. advisement   B. belligerence
    C. guardianship   D. suspicion

    33.___

34. DEBILITY

    A. deceitfulness   B. decency
    C. strength   D. weakness

    34.___

35. DEPLETE

    A. beg   B. empty   C. excuse   D. fold

    35.___

36. ENUMERATE

    A. name one by one   B. disappear
    C. get rid of   D. pretend

    36.___

37. FEIGN

    A. allow   B. incur   C. pretend   D. weaken

    37.___

38. INSTIGATE

    A. analyze   B. coordinate   C. oppose   D. provoke

    38.___

39. LIABLE

    A. careless   B. growing
    C. mistaken   D. responsible

    39.___

40. PONDER

    A. attack   B. heavy   C. meditate   D. solicit

    40.___

41. PUGILIST

    A. farmer   B. politician
    C. prize fighter   D. stage actor

    41.___

42. QUELL

    A. explode   B. inform   C. shake   D. suppress

    42.___

43. RECIPROCAL

    A. mutual   B. organized   C. redundant   D. thoughtful

    43.___

44. RUSE

    A. burn   B. impolite   C. rot   D. trick

    44.___

45. STEALTHY

    A. crazed   B. flowing   C. sly   D. wicked

    45.___

Questions 46-50.

DIRECTIONS: Each of the sentences numbered 46 through 50 may be classified under one of the following four categories:
   A.   faulty because of incorrect grammar
   B.   faulty because of incorrect punctuation
   C.   faulty because of incorrect capitalization or incorrect spelling
   D.   correct
Examine each sentence carefully to determine under which of the above four options it is best classified. Print the letter of the option in the space at the right which is the BEST of the four suggested above. Each faulty sentence contains but one type of error. Consider a sentence to be correct if it contains none of the types of errors mentioned, even though there may be other correct ways of expressing the same thought.

46.   They told both he and I that the prisoner had escaped.   46.____

47.   Any superior officer, who, disregards the just complaints of his subordinates, is remiss in   47.____
the performance of his duty.

48.   Only those members of the national organization who resided in the Middle west   48.____
attended the conference in Chicago.

49.   We told him to give the investigation assignment to whoever was available.   49.____

50.   Please do not disappoint and embarass us by not appearing in court.   50.____

51.   Suppose a man falls from a two-story high scaffold and is unconscious.   51.____
You should

   A.   call for medical assistance and avoid moving the man
   B.   get someone to help you move him indoors to a bed
   C.   have someone help you walk him around until he revives
   D.   hold his head up and pour a stimulant down his throat

52.   For proper first aid treatment, a person who has fainted should be   52.____

   A.   doused with cold water and then warmly covered
   B.   given artificial respiration until he is revived
   C.   laid down with his head lower than the rest of his body
   D.   slapped on the face until he is revived

53.   If you are called on to give first aid to a person who is suffering from shock, you should   53.____

   A.   apply cold towels   B.   give him a stimulant
   C.   keep him awake   D.   wrap him warmly

54.   Artificial respiration would NOT be proper first aid for a person suffering from   54.____

   A.   drowning   B.   electric shock
   C.   external bleeding   D.   suffocation

55. Suppose you are called on to give first aid to several victims of an accident. FIRST attention should be given to the one who is

 A. bleeding severely   B. groaning loudly
 C. unconscious   D. vomiting

 55.__

56. If an officer's weekly salary is increased from $480 to $540, then the percent of increase is _____ percent.

 A. 10   B. 11 1/9   C. 12 1/2   D. 20

 56.__

57. Suppose that one-half the officers in a department have served for more than ten years, and one-third have served for more than 15 years.
Then, the fraction of officers who have served between ten and fifteen years is

 A. 1/3   B. 1/5   C. 1/6   D. 1/12

 57.__

58. In a city prison, there are four floors on which prisoners are housed. The top floor houses one-quarter of the inmates, the bottom floor houses one-sixth of the inmates, one-third are housed on the second floor. The rest of the inmates are housed on the third floor.
If there are 90 inmates housed on the third floor, the TOTAL number of inmates housed on all four floors together is

 A. 270   B. 360   C. 450   D. 540

 58.__

59. Suppose that ten percent of those who commit serious crimes are convicted and that fifteen percent of those convicted are sentenced for more than 3 years.
The percentage of those committing serious crimes who are sentenced for more than 3 years is _____ percent.

 A. 15   B. 1.5   C. .15   D. .015

 59.__

60. Assume that there are 1,100 employees in a city agency. Of these, 15 percent are officers, 80 percent of whom are attorneys. Of the attorneys, two-fifths have been with the agency over five years.
Then, the number of officers who are attorneys and have over five years' experience with the agency is MOST NEARLY

 A. 45   B. 53   C. 132   D. 165

 60.__

61. An employee who has 500 cartons of supplies to pack can pack them at the rate of 50 an hour. After this employee has worked for half an hour, he is joined by another employee who can pack 45 cartons an hour.
Assuming that both employees can maintain their respective rates of speed, then the TOTAL number of hours required to pack all the cartons is

 A. 4 1/2   B. 5   C. 5 1/2   D. 6 1/2

 61.__

62. Thirty-six officers can complete an assignment in 22 days. Assuming that all officers work at the same rate of speed, the number of officers that would be needed to complete this assignment in 12 days is

 A. 42   B. 54   C. 66   D. 72

 62.__

Questions 63-65.

DIRECTIONS: Questions 13 through 15 are to be answered on the basis of the following table. Data for certain categories have been omitted from the table. You are to calculate the missing numbers if needed to answer the questions.

	2005	2006	Numerical Increase
Correction Officers	1,226	1,347	34
Court Attendants		529	
Deputy Sheriffs	38	40	
Supervisors			
	2,180	2,414	-

63. The number in the *Supervisors* group in 2005 was MOST NEARLY   63.____

    A. 500   B. 475   C. 450   D. 425

64. The LARGEST percentage increase from 2005 to 2006 was in the group of   64.____

    A. Court Officers   B. Court Attendants
    C. Deputy Sheriffs   D. Supervisors

65. In 2006, the ratio of the number of Court Officers to the total of the other three categories of employees was MOST NEARLY   65.____

    A. 1:1   B. 2:1   C. 3:1   D. 4:1

66. A directed verdict is made by a court when   66.____

    A. the facts are not disputed
    B. the defendant's motion for a directed verdict has been denied
    C. there is no question of law involved
    D. neither party has moved for a directed verdict

67. Papers on appeal of a criminal case do NOT include one of the following: 67.____

    A. Summons
    B. Minutes of trial
    C. Complaint
    D. Intermediate motion papers

68. A pleading titled *Smith vs. Jones, et. al.* indicates   68.____

    A. two plaintiffs
    B. two defendants
    C. more than two defendants
    D. unknown defendants

69. A District Attorney makes a *prima facie* case when   69.____

    A. there is proof of guilt beyond a reasonable doubt
    B. the evidence is sufficient to convict in the absence of rebutting evidence
    C. the prosecution presents more evidence than the defense
    D. the defendant fails to take the stand

70. A person is NOT qualified to act as a trial juror in a criminal action if he or she   70.___

    A. has been convicted previously of a misdemeanor
    B. is under 18 years of age
    C. has scruples against the death penalty
    D. does not own property of a value at least $500

71. A court clerk who falsifies a court record commits a(n)   71.___

    A. misdemeanor
    B. offense
    C. felony
    D. no crime, but automatically forfeits his tenure

72. Insolent and contemptuous behavior to a judge during a court of record proceeding is   72.___
punishable as

    A. civil contempt   B. criminal contempt
    C. disorderly conduct   D. a disorderly person

73. Offering a bribe to a court clerk would not constitute a crime UNLESS the   73.___

    A. court clerk accepted the bribe
    B. bribe consisted of money
    C. bribe was given with intent to influence the court clerk in his official functions
    D. court was actually in session

74. A defendant comes to trial in the same court in which he had previously been defendant   74.___
in a similar case.
The court officer should

    A. tell him, *knew we'd be seeing you again*
    B. tell newspaper reporters what he knows of the previous action
    C. treat him the same as he would any other defendant
    D. warn the judge that the man had previously been a defendant

75. Suppose in conversation with you, an attorney strongly criticizes a ruling of the judge and   75.___
you believe the attorney to be correct.
You should

    A. assure him you feel the same way
    B. tell him the judge knows the law
    C. tell him to ask for an exception
    D. refuse to discuss the matter

76. One of the inmates in the institution where you are on duty as correction officer is serving   76.___
a sentence for having molested a small girl.
You should

    A. assume that the man should rightfully be in a mental institution
    B. behave towards this man exactly the same as towards the other inmates
    C. handle this man somewhat more gently because he is not a dangerous criminal
    D. handle this man somewhat roughly because of his contemptible crime

77. Suppose that one inmate attacks another in a washroom in a correctional institution. From this information ONLY, it is safe to infer

    A.   that a knife was used in the attack
    B.   that the attacker was young and strong
    C.   that the washroom was otherwise empty
    D.   none of the foregoing

77.____

78. Suppose that an inmate is found badly beaten and unconscious in a corner of the prison laundry where he is employed.
Of the following, the question which would be MOST useful to a correction officer in questioning other inmates to determine the identity of the attacker is:

    A.   What method of assault was used?
    B.   When did the assault take place?
    C.   Who was the assailant?
    D.   Why was the inmate assaulted?

78.____

79. Of the following circumstances, the one a correction officer should LEAST validly regard with suspicion is a(n)

    A.   inmate not being in his cell during the regular check before *lights-out*
    B.   inmate not reporting to his work assignment and who cannot be found
    C.   visitor's attempt to *sneak* an article to an inmate
    D.   well-dressed young woman coming to see an inmate during visiting hours

79.____

80. Suppose you are the correction officer in charge of a work group of about 15 inmates in the institutional garage. Of the following, the MOST practical way to prevent the inmates from concealing tools and carrying them back to their cells is to

    A.   assign one or more tools to each inmate and hold him responsible for them
    B.   have a definite place for each tool and check to see that it is there at the end of the day
    C.   require inmates to strip each day before they are taken back to their cells
    D.   search each man both at the end and the beginning of each day

80.____

81. An inmate stops you and tells you that international bankers are out to *get* him, that already two attempts have been made on his life, and he now fears that the air he breathes is being poisoned. The inmate is an old man who has been in and out of the institution frequently for such minor offenses as vagrancy, alcoholism, loitering, etc. This man is MOST probably

    A.   a victim of amnesia
    B.   a victim of a persecution complex
    C.   covering up an infraction of the rules
    D.   the object of an international plot

81.____

82. Suppose that while you are off duty and unarmed, you recognize on the street an inmate who escaped from your correctional institution a year ago. Apparently, he does not see or recognize you. During this escape, the inmate had gotten hold of a gun and seriously wounded a correction officer.
The BEST of the following actions for you to take is to

82.____

A. attack and subdue the man immediately
B. engage the man in conversation to make sure of your identification
C. follow the man until you can summon an officer to your aid
D. shout *escaped prisoner* so that passersby will help you

83. Suppose a correction officer, feeling that the sentence given an inmate was unfair, permits him to escape.
On the basis of this information ONLY, it is safe to assume that the

83.___

A. correction officer used poor judgment
B. correction officer was recently appointed
C. inmate had possession of a large sum of money
D. judge passing sentence was unduly harsh

84. Suppose that a correctional institution is specially constructed to be escape-proof. Nevertheless, two inmates escape.
The MOST reasonable conclusion on the basis of this information only is that

84.___

A. goals are not always successfully attained
B. not all correction officers are honest
C. the escapers were helped by confederates outside
D. two heads are more resourceful than one

85. Which one of the following descriptions of an escaped inmate would be MOST effective in helping to recapture him?

85.___

A. Age - 31 years; weight - 168 pounds
B. At time of escape was wearing gray hat, dark overcoat
C. Deep scar running from left ear to chin
D. Height - 5 feet, 9 inches; complexion - sallow

86. Allowing inmates to read newspapers in their spare time is

86.___

A. *desirable* since they should be kept informed of the news
B. *undesirable* since they will read of crimes they can imitate after release
C. *desirable* since the advertisements will make them more ambitious
D. *undesirable* since they will read of prison escapes elsewhere

87. Suppose an inmate commits an infraction in the mess hall. The MAIN reason why a correction officer might wait until he was back in his cell before reprimanding him would be that

87.___

A. he should be given time to reflect on his error
B. it might interfere with his enjoyment of the meal
C. the correction officer is not busy during meal times
D. there are several hundred other inmates in the mess hall

88. Of the following, the MOST important reason why correction officers should see to it that the inmates under their supervision know and understand the rules and regulations of the institution is that

88.___

A. the inmates will become aware of the punishment for each violation
B. the job of the correction officers will be made much easier

C.   unintentional violations of the rules will be reduced
D.   with full understanding there will be no violations

89.   In considering punishment for an infraction of the rules by an inmate, the disciplinary   89.____
board in a correction institution is usually guided MAINLY by the thought that

A.   infractions must be punished whether intentional or unintentional
B.   most infractions are deliberate and only few are unintentional
C.   the aim of punishment is to achieve better individual adjustment of the inmate
D.   the infraction was committed by an individual who is a criminal

90.   *When an inmate commits an infraction of discipline, the disciplinary officer or board shall*   90.____
hold a hearing and recommend disciplinary action.
The punishment that should be reserved for the MOST serious infractions is

A.   a severe reprimand before other inmates
B.   denial of athletic privileges
C.   loss of time off for good behavior
D.   restriction against attending movies

91.   *Parole boards have gradually taken over from the judges the function of specifying terms*   91.____
of imprisonment because they are usually in a better position to perform this task.
The MAIN reason for this is most probably that the parole board

A.   can also consider the inmate's prison record
B.   has closer contact with the inmate
C.   is composed of more than one person
D.   usually includes experts in criminology

92.   *In the selection of books for the library of a correctional institution, emphasis should be*   92.____
placed on diversified material.
The MAIN reason for this is the

A.   desire of most inmates to prepare themselves for vocations
B.   fact that most inmates come from urban areas
C.   interest displayed by most inmates in western fiction
D.   various age groups and interests of the inmates

93.   Unscheduled or inconstant patrols by officers will frustrate any planned attempt at irregu-   93.____
larity on the part of inmates.
According to the preceding statement, it is MOST reasonable to assume that

A.   an officer should carefully follow his patrol schedule
B.   inmates should be taught regularity in their activities
C.   officers should make their patrol intentions known to inmates
D.   the element of surprise should be used by officers in their patrols

94.   Generally, the prospect of rehabilitating juvenile delinquents is considerably dimmed by   94.____
throwing them into the same hopper of criminal procedures and institutions as the adult
criminals. Yet, it is a fact that some juvenile offenders are more contaminated by contact
with some of their peers than by contact with adult offenders.
On the basis of the preceding statement, it would be MOST desirable in the correctional treatment of juvenile offenders to

A. classify and segregate all prisoners into groups on the sole basis of type of crime they have committed in order to assure that no undesirable contacts will take place
B. recognize no distinction between juvenile and adult offenders and allow them to mingle throughout the custodial and correctional procedures
C. separate only those adult offenders guilty of the most serious crimes from the general prisoner group and allow the others, adult and juveniles, to mingle throughout the correctional and custodial procedures
D. separate the adults from the juveniles but also further separate the juveniles into groups according to their characteristics

95. It is a frequent misconception that correction officers can be recruited from those registers established for the recruitment of city police or firemen. While it is true that many common qualifications are found in all of these, specific standards for correctional institution work are indicated, varying with the size, geographical location and policies of the institution.
According to this paragraph only, it may be BEST be inferred that

95.____

A. a successful correction officer must have some qualifications not required of a policeman or fireman
B. qualifications which make a successful patrolman will also make a successful fireman
C. the same qualifications are required of a correction officer regardless of the institution to which he is assigned
D. the successful correction officer is required to be both more intelligent and stronger than a fireman

96. A correction officer shall not receive a gift from any inmate or other person on the inmate's behalf.
The BEST explanation for this rule is that

96.____

A. acceptance of a gift has no significance
B. favors may be expected in return
C. inmates cannot usually afford gifts
D. gifts are only an expression of good will

97. Correction officers who deal with the inmate who is a habitual offender should have no false impressions about his character. While extending him a square deal, they should always consider him a source of danger.
According to this statement ONLY, correction officers should deal with inmates who are habitual offenders

97.____

A. carefully and fairly
B. courageously and with self-reliance
C. tolerantly and honestly
D. understandingly and with sympathy

98. Regulations do not permit a correction officer to fire a revolver except when absolutely necessary.
On the basis of this information only, it may be MOST reasonably inferred that

98.____

A. ammunition and bullets are too expensive to be used indiscriminately
B. many correction officers have been dismissed for unnecessary use of firearms
C. the cleaning of a firearm after use is a tedious, time-consuming task
D. the use of a revolver by a correction officer may sometimes be harmful

99. Suppose that a study of inmates at a correctional institution shows that a comparatively small number of first offenders become second offenders, but a very high percentage of second offenders commit further crimes. The MOST reasonable of the following conclusions from this information only is that

    A. the average age of first offenders is considerably less than that of second offenders
    B. it is more difficult to rehabilitate a second offender than a first offender
    C. second offenses are likely to be more serious crimes than first offenses
    D. the term *offender,* as used in the study, is scientifically unacceptable

99.____

100. For the correction officer, the problem of the feebleminded is one of great importance since this group makes up a large proportion of the offenders in any court or institution. Of the following, the one which is NOT a cause of this large proportion of feeble-minded inmates is that

    A. a high percentage of dull offenders are caught and convicted
    B. many dull delinquents come from poor environment
    C. men with low intelligence have natural criminal tendencies
    D. the youth of low intelligence is easily led into crime

100.____

KEY (CORRECT ANSWERS)

1. C	21. D	41. C	61. C	81. B
2. A	22. D	42. D	62. C	82. C
3. B	23. A	43. A	63. D	83. A
4. A	24. C	44. D	64. D	84. A
5. D	25. A	45. C	65. A	85. C
6. A	26. B	46. A	66. A	86. A
7. B	27. C	47. B	67. D	87. D
8. D	28. B	48. C	68. C	88. C
9. D	29. B	49. D	69. B	89. C
10. D	30. D	50. C	70. B	90. C
11. A	31. A	51. A	71. C	91. A
12. B	32. C	52. C	72. B	92. D
13. A	33. C	53. D	73. C	93. D
14. D	34. D	54. C	74. C	94. D
15. A	35. B	55. A	75. D	95. A
16. C	36. A	56. C	76. B	96. B
17. A	37. C	57. C	77. D	97. A
18. D	38. D	58. B	78. C	98. D
19. D	39. D	59. B	79. D	99. B
20. C	40. C	60. B	80. B	100. C

TEST 2

DIRECTIONS: Each question or incomplete statement is followed by several suggested answers or completions. Select the one that BEST answers the question or completes the statement. *PRINT THE LETTER OF THE CORRECT ANSWER IN THE SPACE AT THE RIGHT.*

1. From the standpoint of progressive prison management, it is desirable that the inmates consider the correction officer as a person interested in their welfare rather than as an opponent MAINLY because

    A. a favorable attitude toward the officer on the part of inmates will help in their reha-bilitation
    B. correction officers must perform their duties without regard to the attitudes which they may develop in the inmates
    C. most people expect the correction officer to treat the inmates kindly
    D. prison personnel are now *correction officers* and not *prison guards*

1.___

2. One part of the correction officer's job is to see to it that the inmates obey the rules and regulations of the institution.
To succeed in this part of the job, it would be BEST for the correction officer to

    A. get the inmates to agree with the rules they must obey
    B. get the inmates to understand the need for each rule
    C. see that all the inmates know and understand the rules
    D. stress to the inmates all the penalties for violation of the rules

2.___

3. The man who is a prisoner today was a free man yesterday and will be a free man again tomorrow.
Of the following, the CHIEF significance of this statement for persons engaged in prison work is that

    A. a prisoner should not be treated any better than a person who was never in prison
    B. it is not right to put a man in prison for punishment
    C. prisoners sometimes escape to gain freedom
    D. the prison ought to prepare the inmates for normal living

3.___

4. A correction officer shall immediately notify the Department of any change in address.
Of the following, the BEST reason for this rule is that it

    A. allows for more efficient assignment of correction officers
    B. gives the supervisor a chance to transfer the officer to a new work location if the present one is far from the officer's home
    C. makes it possible to get in touch with the officer quickly in an emergency
    D. makes record keeping within the Department more efficient

4.___

5. Of the following, the crime which a person is LEAST likely to hesitate to commit because of the fear of getting a long prison term is

    A. burglary of a loft   B. embezzlement
    C. robbery of a bank   D. unplanned murder

5.___

6. Two correction officers who had successfully kept a possible riot situation in check were praised by their superior for having shown unusual alertness. The officers commented that they had merely followed the procedures outlined in their CORRECTION OFFICER'S MANUAL.
This incident illustrates that, of the following, the CHIEF value of a good knowledge of their MANUAL for correction officers is that it will help them to

    A. carry out their duties most effectively
    B. develop an original and unique course of action for each new situation
    C. stop possible riots unassisted
    D. understand human nature better

6.____

7. A correctional institution has other functions besides those of good discipline and secure custody.
The one of the following which is LEAST directly related to the functions of good discipline and secure custody is the

    A. fair and consistent treatment of inmates by prison personnel
    B. frequency of careful searches and inspections within the institution
    C. institution's efforts to correct the inmate's antisocial tendencies
    D. institution's regulations to insure safety

7.____

8. Of the following, the MOST important reason for having separate correctional institutions for different types of offenders is that

    A. a smaller staff is required to care for the total prison population when the inmates are separated by type of offense
    B. it is easier to give specialized treatment to offenders of the same type when they are housed in a separate institution
    C. it is less expensive to build several small, specialized institutions than one large, general institution
    D. the judge can sentence the prisoner to a particular institution, relieving the Department of Correction of the responsibility for determining placement

8.____

9. At any particular meal, the average prison inmate is likely to be LEAST concerned with the

    A. amount of meat served at the meal
    B. freshness and cleanliness of the food
    C. nourishment value of the food served
    D. warmth of the food when served

9.____

10. Courts sometimes sentence convicted offenders to an indefinite term, specifying a minimum and a maximum time which is to be served.
Of the following, the CHIEF advantage of this type of indeterminate sentence from a correctional point of view is that

    A. a prisoner can be released sooner if moral improvement is shown
    B. money is saved for the state
    C. the actual time to be served is at the discretion of the judge
    D. the criminal can thereby be convinced to testify for the state

10.____

11. When cloth is purchased to make prison clothing for sentenced inmates, it is LEAST
    important that the cloth

    A. be fairly priced
    B. have good wearing qualities so that it can last a reasonably long time
    C. have stripes of a certain width
    D. present no special problems in cleaning or laundering

12. Of the following, a factor that may make it difficult for released prisoners to *go straight* is
    the fact that

    A. lasting reformation must come from within and cannot be imposed from without
    B. many of their friends and contacts are members of the underworld
    C. scientific advancements have made modern living more pleasant
    D. they are given close supervision by the police for several years

13. It is a post-institutional method of treating offenders outside prison walls.
    The preceding definition describes MOST NEARLY

    A. bail   B. pardon
    C. parole   D. social case work

14. The theory has been advanced that there is, in most cases, a psychological time for the
    release of each prison inmate when the outlook for his rehabilitation is best. Assuming
    this theory to be correct, an important reason why it is difficult to put it into practice is that
    the

    A. follow-up after the inmate's release is as important as his release at the proper
       time
    B. length of an inmate's sentence is set by the judge at the time of sentencing
    C. number of cases where the theory does not hold true is quite large
    D. psychological time is different for each inmate

15. This man must be a correction officer because he wears a uniform.
    This statement is faulty mainly because it assumes that

    A. a man who wears a uniform may be a correction officer
    B. a man who wears a uniform may not be a correction officer
    C. correction officers wear uniforms
    D. only correction officers wear uniforms

16. Black, who is suspected of having stolen some property from Tier A, claims that he could
    not have stolen the property because his cell is in Tier B.
    In order to prove that Black actually could have stolen the property, it is MOST impor-
    tant to know

    A. Black's record at the prison
    B. how long it takes to get from Tier B to Tier A
    C. if Black could get into Tier A
    D. if the stolen property could be of value to Black personally

17. Of the following, the LEAST important reason for censoring incoming mail of prisoners is to   17.____

    A. look for any cash money being sent to prisoners
    B. look for information which may be the key to an escape plot
    C. prevent prisoners from learning of family problems that may worry them
    D. prevent the smuggling of drugs into the prison

18. Progressive prison administrators GENERALLY agree that a recreation program for prison inmates   18.____

    A. has little value in training prisoners to become better citizens
    B. is too expensive to be installed in most prisons
    C. reduces considerably the number of officers needed to guard inmates
    D. should include other activities besides sports

19. It has been found that the better correction officer makes fewer official complaints against inmates for violations of rules.   19.____
Of the following, the MOST probable reason for this is that the better officer

    A. can afford to be more lenient when an inmate commits a violation of the rules
    B. has good control of inmates so that occasions for violations do not arise frequently
    C. is able to punish an inmate without making an official complaint of the violation
    D. knows the proper techniques to use to force inmates to obey the rules

20. A correction officer must take all possible precautions when investigating a fake suicide.   20.____
Of the following, the MOST probable reason for this rule is that

    A. failure by an officer to take all possible precautions when investigating a fake suicide will result in the inmate's death
    B. inmates sometimes pretend to commit suicide merely to place the officer in a position open to attack
    C. the investigation of a suicide is potentially more dangerous to the safety of the officer and the prison than the investigation of many other dangerous situations
    D. there are sometimes unexpected opportunities for committing suicide in a prison

21. Of the following, the MOST important reason why an officer assigned to supervise a large group of inmates eating in a mess hall should be especially alert is that   21.____

    A. all inmates must finish eating in time to report to their work locations
    B. inmates might complain about monotonous or unappetizing food
    C. some inmates might complain that they did not receive equal size portions
    D. very many inmates in the same place at one time is potentially dangerous

22. Suppose that there is a rule which prohibits inmates of a prison from having any cash money in their possession. Of the following, the LEAST important argument in favor of such a rule is that   22.____

    A. it will be easier for inmates to buy things from the prison commissary with cash money
    B. it will reduce stealing of money by one inmate from another
    C. there will be less gambling among inmates
    D. there will be less chance of inmates using cash money to try to bribe employees

23. A correction officer is locking the inmates in their cells for the night.
Of the following, the BEST way for the officer to make sure that no inmate is missing is to

    A. count and identify the inmates before locking them in and then check each cell after locking in
    B. have inmates call out their names as they march past on the way to their cells
    C. have inmates turn in their names and numbers on slips of paper on the way to their cells
    D. line the inmates up, call their names, and check them off as they answer to their names

23._

24. Of the following, the MOST probable reason why a greater number of juvenile delinquents is generally found in a city neighborhood than in a country neighborhood of comparable area is that

    A. a large proportion of the population of cities is made up of *undesirables*
    B. the concentration of population in city areas is generally greater than that in country areas
    C. the educational methods of cities are not as good as those of the country districts
    D. there is greater availability of television, radio, and recreation in city areas

24._

25. When starting to search a prisoner who has been transferred from another institution, a correction officer notices what appear to be a number of small, recently healed punctures in the skin of the prisoner's arm. This discovery should be of significance to the correction officer CHIEFLY as an indication that the prisoner

    A. may have been mistreated at the other institution
    B. should be carefully searched for any instruments of self-mutilation
    C. should be carefully searched for narcotics
    D. should be checked for a history of skin disease

25._

26. A certain correction officer who, upon inspection of a cell, found in it an accumulation of past issues of newspapers, removed all but one or two newspapers from the cell.
The action of this officer was

    A. *good* because such an accumulation is a potential fire hazard
    B. *poor* because it deprives the inmate of a form of recreation
    C. *good* because the normal interval of time between inspections should be reduced
    D. *poor* because the officer could give the extra issues to other inmates

26._

27. Prisoners awaiting trial are not permitted to have razors. Of the following, the MOST important reason for such a rule is that

    A. an inmate who cuts himself with a razor could hold the institution responsible for the injury
    B. inmates have no means of buying razors
    C. razors may be turned into dangerous weapons
    D. trial prisoners are held for such a short time that they do not need shaves

27._

28. Suppose there is a rule that a police officer cannot interview an inmate at the prison unless he presents Form DD-22 from the Police Department. While you are on duty, a detective asks to interview an inmate but claims he left the Form DD-22 at the precinct. Of the following, the BEST action for you to take is to

    28.____

    A. ask him to be sure to get the Form DD-22 and bring it to you immediately after he finishes interviewing the inmate
    B. call the precinct to find out if he left the Form DD-22 there and, if so, permit him to interview the inmate
    C. check his official identification to be sure he is a detective, then permit him to interview the inmate
    D. refuse to permit him to interview the inmate until he presents Form DD-22

29. Suppose that a thief assumes a new name in order to prevent law enforcement agencies from finding out who he really is.
The assumed name is usually referred to as a(n)

    29.____

    A. misnomer   B. alias
    C. alibi   D. nom de plume

30. Of the following, the MAIN difference in organization or function between the Police Department and the Department of Correction is that the Police Department

    30.____

    A. catches criminals whereas the Department of Correction keeps them in jail
    B. has a semi-military type of organization whereas the Department of Correction has a civilian set-up
    C. is headed by a Commissioner whereas a Board of Correction is at the head of the Department of Correction
    D. is subject to State supervision whereas the Department of Correction is not

31. Custody in prison work used to be considered of such supreme importance that everything else was secondary. This statement implies MOST directly that

    31.____

    A. formerly nothing was as important as custody in prison work
    B. formerly only custody was considered important in prison work
    C. today all aspects of prison work are considered equally important
    D. today reform of the prisoner is considered more important than custody

32. Since the total inmate treatment and training program is conditioned largely by custody requirements, its success is almost wholly dependent on flexibility of custody classification and handling of prisoners.
Of the following, the MOST accurate statement based on the preceding statement is that the

    32.____

    A. conditions of custody are completely dependent on the handling of inmates in accordance with their classification
    B. daily schedule at the institution should be flexible in order for the treatment and training program to succeed
    C. main factor influencing the inmate treatment and training program is the requirement for the proper safekeeping of inmates
    D. most important factor in the success of the treatment and training program is the cooperation of the inmates

33. As the fundamental changes sought to be brought about in the inmates of a correctional institution can be accomplished only under good leadership, it follows that the quality of the staff, whose duty it is to influence and guide the inmates in the right direction, is more important than the physical facilities of the institution.
Of the following, the MOST accurate conclusion based on the preceding statement is that

    A. the development of leadership is the fundamental change brought about in inmates by good quality staff
    B. the physical facilities of an institution are not very important in bringing about fundamental changes in the inmates
    C. with proper training, the entire staff of a correctional institution can be developed into good leaders
    D. without good leadership, the basic changes desired in the inmates of a correctional institution cannot be brought about

33.____

34. Prisoners who are receiving decent food and humane treatment and who are busily engaged in useful work programs, carefully organized and purposeful leisure time activities, and self-improvement, rarely resort to disturbances or escape attempts.
The one of the following that is NOT mentioned in the preceding statement as a factor in reducing escape attempts by prisoners is a

    A. program of productive employment
    B. proper classification program
    C. proper feeding program
    D. systematized recreation program

34.____

35. Physical punishment of prison inmates has been shown by experience not only to be ineffective but to be dangerous and, in the long run, destructive of good discipline.
According to the preceding statement, it is MOST reasonable to assume that, in the supervision of prison inmates,

    A. a good correction officer would not use physical punishment
    B. it is permissible for a good correction officer to use a limited amount of physical punishment to enforce discipline
    C. physical punishment improves discipline temporarily
    D. the danger of public scandal is basic in cases where physical punishment is used

35.____

36. There is no clear evidence that criminals, as a group, differ from non-criminals in their basic psychological needs.
On the basis of this statement, it is MOST reasonable to assume that criminals and non-criminals

    A. are alike in some important respects
    B. are alike in their respective backgrounds
    C. differ but slightly in all respects
    D. differ in physical characteristics

36.____

37. Neither immediate protection for the community nor long-range reformation of the prisoner can be achieved by prison personnel who express toward the offender whatever feelings of frustration, fear, jealousy, or hunger for power they may have.
Of the following, the CHIEF significance of this statement for correction officers is that, in their daily work, they should

37.____

A. be on the constant lookout for opportunities to prove their courage to inmates
B. not allow deeply personal problems to affect their relations with the inmates
C. not try to advance themselves on the job because of personal motives
D. spend a good part of their time examining their own feelings in order to understand better those of the inmates

38. Since ninety-five percent of prison inmates are released, and a great majority of these within two to three years, a prison which does nothing more than separate the criminal from society offers little promise of real protection to society.
Of the following, the MOST valid reference which may be drawn from the preceding statement is that

    A. once it has been definitely established that a person has criminal tendencies, that person should be separated for the rest of his life from ordinary society
    B. prison sentences in general are much too short and should be lengthened to afford greater protection to society
    C. punishment, rather than separation of the criminal from society, should be the major objective of a correctional system
    D. when a prison system produces no change in prisoners, and the period of imprisonment is short, the period during which society is protected is also short

38._____

39. A great handicap to successful correctional work lies in the negative response of the general community to the offender. Public attitudes of hostility toward, and rejection of, an ex-prisoner can undo the beneficial effects of even an ideal correctional system.
Of the following, the CHIEF implication of this statement is that

    A. a friendly community attitude will insure the successful reformation of the ex-prisoner
    B. correctional efforts with most prisoners would generally prove successful if it were not for public hostility toward the former inmate
    C. in the long-run, even an ideal correctional system cannot successfully reform criminals
    D. the attitude of the community toward an ex-prisoner is an important factor in determining whether or not an ex-prisoner reforms

39._____

40. While retribution and deterrence as a general philosophy in correction are widely condemned, no one raises any doubt as to the necessity for secure custody of some criminals.
Of the following, the MOST valid conclusion based on the preceding statement is that the

    A. gradual change in the philosophy of correction has not affected custody practices
    B. need for safe custody of some criminals is not questioned by anyone
    C. philosophy of retribution, as shown in some correctional systems, has led to wide condemnation of custodial practices applied to all types of criminals
    D. practice of secure custody of some criminals is the result of society's desire for retribution and deterrence

40._____

Questions 41-42.

DIRECTIONS: Questions 41 and 42 are to be answered on the basis of the following paragraph.

*Those correction theorists who are in agreement with severe and rigid controls as a nor-
mal part of the correctional process are confronted with a contradiction; this is so because a
responsibility which is consistent with freedom cannot be developed in a repressive atmosphere. They do not recognize this contradiction when they carry out their programs with dictatorial force and expect convicted criminals exposed to such programs to be reformed into
free and responsible citizens.*

41. According to the above paragraph, those correction theorists are faced with a contradiction who

  A. are in favor of the enforcement of strict controls in a prison
  B. believe that to develop a sense of responsibility, freedom must not be restricted
  C. take the position that the development of responsibility consistent with freedom is
    not possible in a repressive atmosphere
  D. think that freedom and responsibility can be developed only in a democratic atmo-
    sphere

41.___

42. According to the above paragraph, a repressive atmosphere in a prison

  A. does not conform to present day ideas of freedom of the individual
  B. is admitted by correction theorists to be in conflict with the basic principles of the
    normal correctional process
  C. is advocated as the best method of maintaining discipline when rehabilitation is of
    secondary importance
  D. is not suitable for the development of a sense of responsibility consistent with free-
    dom

42.___

43. To state the matter in simplest terms, just as surely as some people are inclined to commit crimes, so some people are prevented from committing crimes by the fear of the consequences to themselves.
Of the following, the MOST logical conclusion based on this statement is that

  A. as many people are prevented from committing criminal acts as actually commit
    criminal acts
  B. most men are not inclined to commit crimes
  C. people who are inclined to violate the law are usually deterred from their purpose
  D. there are people who have a tendency to commit crimes and people who are
    deterred from crime

43.___

44. Probation is a judicial instrument whereby a judge may withhold execution of a sentence
upon a convicted person in order to give opportunity for rehabilitation in the community
under the guidance of an officer of the court. According to the preceding statement, it is
MOST reasonable to assume that

  A. a person on probation must report to the court at least once a month
  B. a person who has been convicted of crime is sometimes placed on probation by
    the judge

44.___

C. criminals who have been rehabilitated in the community are placed on probation by the court after they are sentenced
D. the chief purpose of probation is to make the sentence easier to serve

Questions 45-47.

DIRECTIONS: Questions 45 through 47 are to be answered on the basis of the information contained in the following paragraph.

Group counseling may contain potentialities of an extraordinary character for the philosophy and especially the management and operation of the adult correctional institution. Primarily, the change may be based upon the valued and respected participation of the rank-and-file of employees in the treatment program. Group counseling provides new treatment functions for correctional workers. The older, more conventional duties and activities of correctional officers, teachers, maintenance foremen and other employees, which they currently perform, may be fortified and improved by their participation in group counseling. Psychologists, psychiatrists, and classification officers may also need to revise their attitudes toward others on the staff and toward their own procedure in treating inmates to accord with the new type of treatment program which may evolve if group counseling were to become accepted practice in the prison. The primary locale of the psychological treatment program may move from the clinical center to all places in the institution where inmates are in contact with employees. The thoughtful guidance and steering of the program, figuratively its pilot-house, may still be the clinical center. The actual points of contact of the treatment program will, however, be wherever inmates are in personal relationship, no matter how superficial, with employees of the prison.

45. According to the above paragraph, a basic change that may be brought about by the introduction of a group counseling program into an adult correctional institution would be that the   45._____

   A. educational standards for correctional employees would be raised
   B. management of the institution would have to be selected primarily on the basis of ability to understand and apply the counseling program
   C. older and conventional duties of correctional employees would assume less importance
   D. rank-and-file employees would play an important part in the treatment program for inmates

46. According to the above paragraph, the one of the following that is NOT mentioned specifically as a change that may be required by or result from the introduction of group counseling in an adult correctional institution is a change in the   46._____

   A. attitude of the institution's classification officers toward their own procedures in treating inmates
   B. attitudes of the institution's psychologists toward correction officers
   C. place where the treatment program is planned and from which it is directed
   D. principal place where the psychological treatment program makes actual contact with the inmate

47. According to the above paragraph, under a program of group counseling in an adult correctional institution, treatment of inmates takes place

A. as soon as they are admitted to the prison
B. chiefly in the clinical center
C. mainly where inmates are in continuing close and personal relationship with the technical staff
D. wherever inmates come in contact with prison employees

47.___

Questions 48-50.

DIRECTIONS: Questions 48 and 50 are to be answered on the basis of the information contained in the following paragraph.

As a secondary aspect of this revolutionary change in outlook resulting from the introduction of group counseling into the adult correctional institution, there must evolve a new type of prison employee, the true correctional or treatment worker. The top management will have to reorient their attitudes toward subordinate employees, respecting and accepting them as equal participants in the work of the institution. Rank may no longer be the measure of value in the inmate treatment program. Instead, the employee will be valuable whatever his location in the prison hierarchy or administrative plan in terms of his capacity constructively to relate himself to inmates as one human being to another. In group counseling, all employees must consider it their primary task to provide a wholesome environment for personality growth for the inmates in work crews, cell blocks, clerical pools or classrooms. The above does not mean that custodial care and precautions regarding the prevention of disorders or escapes are cast aside or discarded by prison workers. On the contrary, the staff will be more acutely aware of the costs to the inmates of such infractions of institutional rules. Gradually, it is hoped, these instances of uncontrolled responses to over-powering feelings by inmates will become much less frequent in the treatment institution. In general, men in group counseling provide considerably fewer disciplinary infractions when compared with a control group of those still on a waiting list to enter group counseling, and especially fewer than those who do not choose to participate. It is optimistically anticipated that some day men in prison may have the same attitudes toward the staff, the same security in expecting treatment as do patients in a good general hospital.

48. According to the above paragraph, under a program of group counseling in an adult correctional institution, that employee will be MOST valuable in the inmate treatment program who

A. can establish a constructive relationship of one human being to another between himself and the inmate
B. gets top management to accept him as an equal participant in the work of the institution
C. is in contact with the inmate in work crews, cell blocks, clerical pools or classrooms
D. provides the inmate with a proper home environment for wholesome personality growth

48.___

49. According to the above paragraph, an effect that the group counseling program is expected to have on the problem of custody and discipline in a prison is that the staff will

    49.____

    A. be more acutely aware of the cost of maintaining strict prison discipline
    B. discard old and outmoded notions of custodial care and the prevention of disorders and escapes
    C. neglect this aspect of prison work unless proper safeguards are established
    D. realize more deeply the harmful effect on the inmate of breaches of discipline

50. According to the above paragraph, a result that is expected from the group counseling method of inmate treatment in an adult correctional institution is

    50.____

    A. a greater desire on the part of potential delinquents to enter the correctional institution for the purpose of securing treatment
    B. a large reduction in the number of infractions of institutional rules by inmates
    C. a steady decrease in the crime rate
    D. the introduction of hospital methods of organization and operation into the correctional institution

KEY (CORRECT ANSWERS)

1. A	11. C	21. D	31. A	41. A
2. C	12. B	22. A	32. C	42. D
3. D	13. C	23. A	33. D	43. D
4. C	14. B	24. B	34. B	44. B
5. D	15. D	25. C	35. A	45. D
6. A	16. C	26. A	36. A	46. C
7. C	17. C	27. C	37. B	47. D
8. B	18. D	28. D	38. D	48. A
9. C	19. B	29. B	39. D	49. D
10. A	20. B	30. A	40. B	50. B

EXAMINATION SECTION
TEST 1

DIRECTIONS: Each question or incomplete statement is followed by several suggested answers or completions. Select the one that BEST answers the question or completes the statement. *PRINT THE LETTER OF THE CORRECT ANSWER IN THE SPACE AT THE RIGHT.*

1. Of the following, it is MOST important that a newly appointed correction officer be   1._____

    A. intelligent
    B. thoroughly informed on the latest correctional techniques
    C. unafraid of anything
    D. very strong

2. The correction officer's attitude toward the prisoners supervised should be very   2._____

    A. friendly   B. impartial
    C. suspicious   D. tough

3. Of the following, the BEST reason for separating first offenders from habitual offenders in   3._____
    a prison is that

    A. contact with hardened inmates may be harmful to the first offender
    B. first offenders may object to being housed with other criminals
    C. first offenders should be sent to reformatories rather than confined in a prison
    D. individual attention should be given to every inmate

4. Of the following, the LEAST important reason for sending law violators to prison is to   4._____

    A. discourage them from committing more crimes in the future
    B. punish them for their violation of the law
    C. remove them from the influence of society
    D. warn other possible offenders that crime does not pay

5. John Jones, who has a long record of juvenile delinquency, is the son of Robert Jones   5._____
    who has a long criminal record. The one of the following which has probably contributed
    LEAST to making John a juvenile delinquent is

    A. growth in a poor environment
    B. hero worship
    C. inherited criminal traits
    D. parental neglect

6. Suppose that studies show that 15% of all prison inmates have had no schooling, 67.5%   6._____
    have attended elementary school only, 14.5% have attended high school, and 3% have
    had some college.
    On the basis of this data, it is MOST reasonable to assume that

    A. a smaller percentage of college graduates than of high school graduates commit
       crimes
    B. educational attainment is related to crime as depression is related to unemploy-
       ment

    C.   educational opportunities have increased but crime has not decreased
    D.   people with little education make up the greatest part of the general prison population

7.   Of the following, the MAIN reason why it is desirable for a correction officer to know the criminal history of the inmates supervised is that   7.___

    A.   an inmate's criminal history is a factor influencing the type of custodial supervision the officer must give
    B.   the inmates will be favorably impressed with the officer's knowledge of the job
    C.   the officer may be called upon to testify in court about these inmates
    D.   while many inmates are confined in the one prison, no two inmates will have the same criminal history

8.   Sometimes a person who has just been charged with a crime is kept in jail until the trial comes up. The relationship established between the correction officer and such a prisoner who has just been admitted and is waiting to be tried is very important MAINLY because this class of prisoner is usually   8.___

    A.   aware of the need to abide by prison regulations
    B.   emotionally upset because of imprisonment
    C.   in need of legal advice from the correction officer
    D.   most likely to try to win favor with the correction officer

9.   Of the following, the CHIEF value of a brief introductory training course for newly appointed correction officers is that such a course can   9.___

    A.   give the new employee an introduction to the basic aspects of the correction officer's job
    B.   give the new employees a thorough knowledge of the main principles of correctional theory and practice
    C.   point up the relationship of the correction department to other government agencies
    D.   serve as an additional test of the employees' fitness for the position

10.   Suppose you have reason to believe that there is contraband hidden in one or more of the cells on your post. However, after making a quick search, you have been unable to find any contraband.
Of the following, the BEST action for you to take is to   10.___

    A.   forget about the matter; as your search has failed to locate any contraband, you were probably mistaken
    B.   keep on the alert for a few months until you catch an inmate using contraband
    C.   recommend to your captain that a thorough search of the post be organized
    D.   search the suspected cells again at some time in the future

11.   Suppose that you are transferred to a post that has been supervised by another officer for a few years. The daily post routine established by this officer is very different from the one that you would prefer to use.
In this situation, it would be MOST desirable for you to   11.___

A. immediately adopt your own routine so that the inmates will know what to expect
B. introduce changes in routine gradually so that the inmates under your supervision will not be confused
C. let the routine established by the other officer continue unchanged as it has taken a long time to build up
D. make up a new routine consisting of about fifty percent of procedures used by the other officer and fifty percent of procedures that you favor

12. Suppose that a civilian employee of the prison commissary comes to your post to sell small articles to the inmates. The inmates have crowded around the commissary employee, and the selling is taking place in a very disorderly and noisy manner.
Of the following, the MOST desirable action for you to take is to

   12.____

A. arrange the inmates in a line and have the commissary items sold to them in line order
B. contact the commissary office and ask them to send up another employee to help with the selling
C. help the commissary employee yourself with the selling so that the inmates can be taken care of more quickly
D. stop the sale of commissary items and tell the commissary employee to come back another time

13. Suppose that the rules of the prison do not allow a prisoner to carry more than a certain amount of cash at any one time. One day you find that a prisoner on your post is carrying more than the allowable amount of cash. Of the following, the BEST action for you to take would be to

   13.____

A. have the prisoner turn over the extra cash to you and submit it to your superior with a report
B. issue a warning to the prisoner against further violations of this rule in the future
C. say nothing to the prisoner but keep a close watch to see if the money is spent
D. take away the extra cash and keep it until the prisoner is released

14. Suppose that while you are on duty alone in a mess hall where a fairly large number of inmates are having supper, two inmates walk over to you and in a loud and insulting manner demand more food, claiming that some of their food is spoiled.
Of the following, it would be MOST desirable for you to

   14.____

A. give the inmates more food but report them to your superior for disciplinary action after they have been returned to their cells
B. order the inmates back to their table, using force if necessary
C. order the inmates out of the mess hall and back to the cell tier
D. tell the inmates that you will give them more food from the kitchen only if they agree to pay for it later

15. Suppose that an inmate on your post is afraid of an attack by certain other inmates of the cell tier.
Of the following, the BEST action for you to take is to

   15.____

A. announce at the next inmate roll call that assault is a misdemeanor even if committed in prison
B. discuss with your immediate superior the advisability of moving this inmate to another floor in the institution

    C.   immediately take this inmate to see the head of the prison
    D.   tell the inmate not to be afraid as there is always an officer on guard

16. Suppose that you are in charge of a work gang made up of inmates from different tiers and floors of the prison. Upon taking a count after the work gang is assembled one morning, you find that one prisoner has not yet reported. Of the following, the BEST action for you to take is to   16.___

    A.   immediately begin a search for the missing prisoner with the help of the other inmates of the work gang
    B.   notify the head of the prison
    C.   report this fact by telephone to the officer in command of the tier to which the missing inmate is assigned
    D.   sound a general alarm

17. One day you take a count of the inmates of your cell block after they return from mess and find that you are one inmate over.
Of the following, the BEST action for you to take is to   17.___

    A.   ask that anyone who does not belong in this group step forward and let this inmate return to the proper tier
    B.   assign the extra inmate to a cell and wait until the inmate is reported missing
    C.   call the roll of the inmates, ask if the name of any inmate has not been called, and then let this inmate return to the proper tier
    D.   personally identify each inmate against your records in order to first make sure who the extra inmate is

18. A correction officer is alone with a group of inmates at work when two of the inmates start a fight. The officer immediately steps in and tries to separate the two inmates by force. This action is   18.___

    A.   *desirable* because it keeps the fight from spreading
    B.   *desirable* because it shows the inmates that the officer is not afraid
    C.   *undesirable* because it is preferable to let the two inmates fight it out rather than to let the other inmates get out of control
    D.   *undesirable* because the officer should first call for assistance before taking any further action

19. Of the following, the MAIN reason why it is generally undesirable for a correction officer to reprimand an inmate in front of other inmates is that   19.___

    A.   discipline should be thought out before it is applied
    B.   embarrassment may make the inmate resentful and create problems of supervision for the officer
    C.   the officer should not hesitate to show the other inmates that he is always in command of the situation
    D.   the other inmates may object to the officer's action because they consider it to be unwarranted

20. Suppose that you are informed by Inmate X that the prisoners on your post have made plans to stage a riot in the mess hall the next day.
Of the following, the BEST action for you to take is to

    A. be especially on the alert the next day so as to forestall any riot that may be planned before it gets started
    B. have the probable ringleaders fed in their cells the next day
    C. line up the inmates, tell them you have received certain information from Inmate X, and warn them against any forbidden demonstrations
    D. notify your commanding officer who will make a decision as to what should be done

20._____

21. A correction officer is justified in using physical force against an inmate

    A. in self-defense
    B. under no circumstances
    C. when no weapons are at hand
    D. when provoked by an inmate

21._____

22. When entering a cell occupied by an inmate to investigate a suspicious circumstance, a correction officer should be accompanied by another officer.
This recommendation is

    A. *sound* because additional protection is afforded in the event of sudden attack
    B. *sound* because additional witnesses to suspicious circumstances must always be produced
    C. *unsound* because it is wasteful of staff
    D. *unsound* because serious delay will occur if another officer is not immediately available

22._____

23. Reading of newspapers, books, or other materials by a correction officer while on duty is prohibited.
Of the following, the BEST justification for this rule is that the

    A. material read cannot be thoroughly understood if proper attention is given to required matters
    B. officer reading on post will impress unfavorably official and other visitors
    C. officer should give undivided attention to the responsibilities of the post
    D. only newspapers and books which relate to correctional work should be read by the officer while on duty

23._____

24. Of the following, the MAIN reason why it is very important that all eating utensils be carefully accounted for after each meal by prison inmates is that

    A. accounting for such utensils should not be the responsibility of the kitchen staff alone
    B. such utensils can sometimes be used as weapons by inmates
    C. the steady loss of such utensils adds too much to the cost of prison operation
    D. the use of such utensils is a privilege and not a right

24._____

25. Of the following, the MAIN reason why a material witness to a crime is sometimes kept in jail until the trial of the accused is over is that the   25.__

    A. danger of the witness being harmed is thereby reduced
    B. evidence may show that the witness is also involved in the crime
    C. law requires it in all cases
    D. witness will be more willing to cooperate with the District Attorney

26. From the point of view of society in general, it is MOST desirable that the diet for prison inmates be   26.__

    A. as inexpensive as possible but tasty, varied, and healthy
    B. of the same level as that of the person of average income outside the prison
    C. the same as that for the prison administration in order to avoid food riots
    D. the very minimum required to maintain life

27. In the institutions of the Department of Correction are kept not only sentenced prisoners but also accused persons awaiting trial.   27.__
Of the following, the MOST probable reason why some accused persons are kept in jail while awaiting trial is that

    A. as the weight of the evidence is against the accused, they must prove their inno-
cence
    B. they have been unable to furnish the bail set by the court
    C. they will be discouraged from giving false testimony at the time of the trial
    D. this makes it easier for the District Attorney to prepare his case

28. Of the following, the MOST probable reason why the years between 18 and 35 have been referred to as *the age of criminality of man* is that   28.__

    A. a person under 18 is classed as a juvenile delinquent while a person over 35 has
established family ties which keep him from criminal activities
    B. most crimes are committed by persons in that age group
    C. most people are exposed to criminal influences during those years
    D. these are the least stable years in the average person's life

29. Studies have shown that most crimes are committed between 9 P.M. and 12 Midnight.   29.__
Of the following, the LEAST probable reason for this is that during these hours there is
a(n)

    A. *decrease* in the chance of being caught
    B. *increase* in business and commerce
    C. *increase* in leisure time
    D. *increase* in social contacts

30. Of the following, the condition that would probably lead to the GREATEST public criticism of the granting of parole to convicted offenders would be the   30.__

    A. coddling of prison inmates
    B. commission of crimes by parolees
    C. interference by politicians in prison management
    D. use of parole with second offenders

31. Of the following, the BEST evidence in support of the theory that fluctuations in the crime rate are not caused by economic conditions alone is the

    A. commission of crimes against property by well-to-do people
    B. decrease in crime accompanying an increase in employment opportunities
    C. higher rate of unemployment among convicted persons
    D. low economic status of convicted offenders

31.____

32. From time to time, there has been public criticism of the practice of providing recreational programs for prison inmates.
Such criticism is

    A. *justified* because if the prison experience is made too pleasant, it will not be an effective crime preventive
    B. *justified* because such programs are an unnecessary expense on the public budget
    C. *unjustified* because such programs are not very expensive
    D. *unjustified* because such programs help to make inmates law-abiding citizens

32.____

33. After they have served a part of their sentence, offenders are released under the continued custody of the state and under conditions that permit their reimprisonment in the event of misbehavior.
The preceding statement defines MOST accurately

    A. bail   B. pardon   C. parole   D. probation

33.____

34. The correction officer plays a very important role in the rehabilitation of the inmate for it is the correction officer who spends the most time with the inmate.
Of the following, the MOST accurate statement based on the preceding statement is that

    A. a great deal of time is required to successfully rehabilitate any inmate
    B. any individual who spends time with inmates can contribute a great deal to their rehabilitation
    C. during the period of imprisonment, the inmate has the greatest amount of contact with the correction officer
    D. most inmates go to the correction officer for guidance

34.____

35. A large proportion of persons in short-term penal institutions are there because of their inability to pay fines.
Of the following, the MOST accurate conclusion based on the preceding statement is that

    A. courts sometimes impose a fine as an alternative to a jail sentence
    B. law violators who are fined are kept in short-term institutions
    C. many fines are for rather large amounts as shown by the inability of the fined person to pay
    D. persons who are sentenced to short-term institutions may, if they do not wish to serve the sentence, pay a fine instead

35.____

36. Good discipline in a prison means an undisturbed procedure so organized that the presence of the executive head may be dispensed with from time to time.
According to the preceding statement, it is MOST reasonable to assume that

    A. if prison routines are disturbed during the absence of the executive head, a breakdown in discipline is sure to result
    B. in a prison where good discipline exists, occasional absences of the warden do not interfere with smooth operation
    C. in a well-organized prison with an established procedure, areas and levels of responsibility are clearly defined and problems of discipline do not exist
    D. the executive head of a prison is not needed if good discipline exists

36.__

37. The distinction in the criminal law of the United States between a misdemeanant and a felon was that the former received a sentence under a year whereas the latter received a sentence of a year or over.

37.__

Of the following, the MOST accurate conclusion based on the preceding statement is that under the criminal law of the United States,
    A. a felony was considered a more serious crime than a misdemeanor
    B. all crimes were classified as misdemeanors or felonies
    C. all persons accused of felonies received sentences of more than a year
    D. some misdemeanants received the same prison sentence as some felons

37.__

38. Paroles may be granted by the board of managers at any time and prisoners are referred to the board for parole consideration whenever the warden and the classification committee believe they have received the maximum benefit from institutional treatment and training and the conditions in the community are relatively favorable.
Of the following, the MOST accurate conclusion based on the preceding statement is that

38.__

    A. a parole, to be valid, must be approved by the classification committee and the board of managers
    B. during periods of economic depression very few paroles are granted because employment conditions in the community are not favorable
    C. prisoners become eligible for parole upon completion of the required minimum part of their sentence, provided their conduct in prison has been satisfactory
    D. prisoners who have not yet benefited from the institutional treatment program are not likely to be referred for parole consideration

39. No other aspect of prison life has invaded the public interest as frequently as the matter of punishment. According to the preceding statement, it is MOST reasonable to assume that the

39.__

    A. extent of public interest in all prison matters is very great
    B. punishment is not the only aspect of prison life that the public has been interested in
    C. punishment of any prison inmate will be criticized by the public whenever it is brought to light
    D. study of the punishment of prison inmates is not an easy task

40. Prison officials have been afraid of the prisoner because they saw him not as a single unit but in his aggregate aspect as the whole population of the institution. According to the preceding statement, it is MOST reasonable to assume that prison officials have been afraid of the prisoner because

    A. during any prison riot every prisoner in the institution is a dangerous individual
    B. each prisoner is representative of any other prisoner
    C. they feared a possible attack by the individual prisoner
    D. they recognized the possible danger of united action by all the prisoners

40.____

41. If a defendant in a lower court is unable to pay the fines and costs, he must usually serve time in the jail or workhouse in order to *work off* the payment at so much per day.
Of the following, the MOST valid conclusion based on the preceding statement is that the

    A. greater the fine in a lower court, the longer the jail sentence that must be served in place thereof
    B. money earned by inmates serving time in a jail or workhouse must be used to pay the fines and costs
    C. sentences in the lower courts are only for a few days
    D. sentences in the lower courts are to jail and workhouses while sentences in the higher courts are to state prisons

41.____

42. In 1997, there were 99,249 inmates confined in penal institutions operated by local juris-dictions, composed mainly of jails and workhouses, whereas there were 217,919 inmates in penal establishments operated by federal and state governments, composed mainly of prisons and reformatories.
According to the preceding statement, in 1997

    A. federal and state governments did not operate jails and workhouses
    B. most inmates were confined in locally operated jails, workhouses, prisons, or refor-matories
    C. the number of inmates in locally operated penal institutions was less than half the number in state and federally operated institutions
    D. the total of more than three hundred thousand inmates confined does not include any inmates confined in local institutions which were not jails and workhouses

42.____

43. Punishment in prison is of two kinds: the infliction of pain or discomfort or the negative aspect, namely, the deprivation of normal comfort or privileges.
According to the preceding statement, it is MOST reasonable to assume that in prison the

    A. deprivation of normal comfort or privileges has a negative effect
    B. deprivation of privileges is a less effective form of punishment than the infliction of pain
    C. infliction of pain or discomfort on a prisoner as a form of punishment brings positive results
    D. taking away from a prisoner the privilege of reading mail is a form of punishment

43.____

44. A feature of present day penology is that most prisoners are eventually released to soci-   44.___
    ety where their success or failure will, in large measure, depend on the calibre of their
    intramural care and treatment and the efficiency of their parole plans and supervision.
    Of the following, the MOST reasonable conclusion based on the preceding statement
    is that

    A. a former prisoner's failure to make a good adjustment after release can sometimes
        be due in part to a poor parole plan
    B. imprisonment and parole have the same objectives
    C. the main objective of present day penology is the release of prisoners back into
        society as soon as possible
    D. with proper care, treatment, and supervision while in prison and when on parole,
        any convict can be successfully restored to society

45. The sentence imposed by the court on a convicted person is a poor indication of the   45.___
    actual time the offender will spend in prison.
    In most cases, this is so MAINLY because

    A. hardened criminals will make successful attempts to escape
    B. the prisoner may be pardoned
    C. the sentence may be reduced by the Governor on recommendation of the District
        Attorney
    D. time off may be earned for good behavior

46. The old prison is gradually being changed into something that might diagnose and treat   46.___
    the prisoners rather than punish them.
    According to the preceding statement,

    A. diagnosis and treatment will succeed whenever punishment fails
    B. the objectives and methods of the prison are being modified
    C. the old prison and the new have very little in common
    D. where diagnosis and treatment fail, punishment must be tried

47. Under the state-use system of prison labor, the state conducts a business of manufac-   47.___
    ture but the use or sale of the goods is limited to the institution where manufactured or to
    other state institutions and agencies.
    According to the preceding statement, under the state-use system of prison labor, the

    A. goods manufactured can be used only by state prisons
    B. products of inmate labor cannot be sold on the open market
    C. state competes with private industry in the manufacture of all those articles which
        are needed to operate a penal institution
    D. variety of articles manufactured is limited to those which can be used in the institu-
        tion where they are made

48. Jails and workhouses take care of an unusually large number of psychopathic and men-   48.____
tally abnormal individuals but the available data do not permit accurate comparisons with
the distribution of mental abnormality in prisons and reformatories.
According to the preceding statement, it is MOST correct to state that

    A. a conclusion on the basis of the available data that there are more or fewer psycho-
pathic individuals in jails than in prisons is likely to be incorrect
    B. a very large number of individuals of abnormal mentality are to be found in prisons
and reformatories
    C. the available data regarding the distribution of mentally abnormal individuals in
penal institutions is inaccurate
    D. the distribution of psychopathic and mentally abnormal individuals in jails and
workhouses cannot be compared with the distribution of such individuals in prisons
and reformatories

49. Penologists are advocating the extension of the indeterminate sentence to the misde-   49.____
meanant group so that the institution can relate the inmate's progress to his release.
According to the preceding statement, it is MOST correct to say that a feature of the
indeterminate sentence is that

    A. an inmate who does not show satisfactory progress can be kept in jail indefinitely
until he is completely rehabilitated
    B. it was first used with the misdemeanant group of prisoners
    C. the time to be served is at least a year but no more than two years
    D. two inmates sentenced for the same class of offense do not necessarily have to
serve the same amount of time

50. Adequate personnel is the first and most important ingredient of a good institutional pro-   50.____
gram.
Of the following, the CHIEF justification of the preceding statement is that

    A. a good institutional program cannot be developed unless the personnel required to
put it into effect has first been assembled
    B. many institutions do not have adequate personnel
    C. the best institutional program is not likely to succeed without the personnel quali-
fied to carry it out
    D. there are several ingredients in a good personnel program

KEY (CORRECT ANSWERS)

1.	A	11.	B	21.	A	31.	A	41.	A
2.	B	12.	A	22.	A	32.	D	42.	C
3.	A	13.	A	23.	C	33.	C	43.	D
4.	C	14.	A	24.	B	34.	C	44.	A
5.	C	15.	B	25.	A	35.	A	45.	D
6.	D	16.	C	26.	A	36.	B	46.	B
7.	A	17.	D	27.	B	37.	A	47.	B
8.	B	18.	D	28.	B	38.	D	48.	A
9.	A	19.	B	29.	B	39.	B	49.	D
10.	C	20.	D	30.	B	40.	D	50.	C

TEST 2

DIRECTIONS: Each question or incomplete statement is followed by several suggested answers or completions. Select the one that BEST answers the question or completes the statement. *PRINT THE LETTER OF THE CORRECT ANSWER IN THE SPACE AT THE RIGHT.*

1. It is recommended that the number of cells in a new prison be determined not by the expected average population of the prison but by the expected maximum.
Of the following, the BEST argument in support of the preceding recommendation is that the

    1.___

    A. average population is of no value as an index of the number of prisoners who are likely to be received at an institution
    B. number of cells in a prison should be as great as possible
    C. prison should be constructed as economically as possible
    D. prison should be equipped to handle the greatest load it is likely to get

2. A crime is nothing more than behavior; it may be one act or a form of conduct which is unacceptable to the organized social group at a given time and in a given place, so unacceptable that the community has prohibited it by law.
According to the preceding statement,

    2.___

    A. an act that is prohibited by law is a crime
    B. behavior which is against the welfare of society is a crime
    C. conduct which is unacceptable to the community constitutes a crime
    D. unacceptable behavior and crime are the same thing

3. Parole has far less potential danger to the public than the unconditional release of an offender at the full expiration of the sentence since it permits a period of close watching with the safeguard of a possible return to the institution if the proper adjustment is not made. According to the preceding statement, it is MOST correct to state that

    3.___

    A. offenders should have a short period of close watching after their release from prison
    B. paroled offenders can be returned to prison under certain conditions
    C. the advantages of parole are more numerous than its disadvantages
    D. the unconditional release of an offender is dangerous to the public

4. Full completions of the sentence means that the final limit of the penalty imposed by the court has been reached and there is no longer any legal authority over the offender in connection with that particular offense. According to the preceding statement, where there is full completion of the sentence,

    4.___

    A. no further punishment or restraint can be imposed by the government for the offense in question
    B. the court has given the maximum penalty permitted under the law and society can no longer impose any legal restrictions on the offender
    C. the full limit of the penalty permitted by law for the offense has not been imposed by the court
    D. there is no longer any legal authority over the former offender

5. The ratio of male to female prisoners received in jails and workhouses is 14 to 1.   5.____
   Of the following, the MOST valid conclusion based on the preceding statement is that

   A. female prisoners constitute one-fourteenth of all the prisoners received in jails and
      workhouses
   B. in any group of prisoners received at a jail or workhouse it is unlikely that there will
      be more than one female prisoner
   C. male prisoners constitute 14 percent of all prisoners received in jails and work-
      houses
   D. on the average, for every 1400 male prisoners received in jails and workhouses,
      100 female prisoners are received

6. Of the following, the MAIN reason why it is preferable to use a sterile rather than a non-   6.____
   sterile dressing directly over a wound is that the sterile dressing is

   A. cheaper
   B. easier for the first aider to make
   C. easier to apply
   D. less likely to contain germs

7. Suppose that an inmate has stopped breathing as the result of an accident.   7.____
   After sending for medical assistance, the correction officer should then immediately

   A. administer a strong drink
   B. begin to rub the victim's hands
   C. place the victim on a bed and cover with blankets
   D. start artificial respiration

8. In dealing with an external wound, the first and most important thing to do is to stop   8.____
   severe bleeding.
   Of the following, the CHIEF justification for this statement is that

   A. death can result from too much loss of blood
   B. external wounds are sometimes more serious than internal wounds
   C. infection will set in if bleeding is not stopped
   D. severe bleeding is evidence that an artery has been cut

9. A correction officer must exercise extreme care in moving an inmate who has just suf-   9.____
   fered a simple fracture MAINLY because of the danger of

   A. causing additional fractures in other bones
   B. increasing the bleeding
   C. the broken bone pushing through the skin
   D. the victim losing consciousness

10. Suppose you believe that an inmate is going to faint. Of the following, the BEST first aid   10.____
    measure for you to take FIRST is to

    A. have the inmate walk up and back briskly
    B. lay the inmate down, head level with or lower than the rest of the body
    C. rub the inmate's hands and arms vigorously
    D. seat the inmate erect in a chair and offer some water or other liquid to drink

11. We should beware of assuming that a new jail necessarily means a good penal institution.
This statement implies MOST directly that

    A. not all good penal institutions are new
    B. not all old jails are bad penal institutions
    C. some new jails are not good penal institutions
    D. some old jails are good penal institutions

11.__

12. A good probation department, by furnishing the judge with information regarding the guilty individual, makes possible discrimination in the use of imprisonment and, in the person of the probation officer, provides a substitute for it.
Of the following, the MOST direct implication of the preceding statement is that

    A. a properly functioning probation department offers the means for effective use of probation in lieu of imprisonment for some offenders
    B. if used with discrimination by the judge, probation is sometimes in itself an indirect form of punishment
    C. probation, as a substitute for imprisonment, should be more widely used
    D. the primary function of a good probation officer is to secure background information about the offender

12.__

13. The fact that the offense is not serious does not mean that the perpetrator can be easily turned into a law-abiding citizen.
Of the following, the BEST evidence in support of this statement is the

    A. high rate of recidivism among misdemeanant prisoners
    B. large number of small jails
    C. number of prisoners who violate parole
    D. reluctance of society to accept the former convict

13.__

14. The chain of prison administration is only as strong as its weakest officer.
The preceding statement implies MOST directly that

    A. careful selection and proper training of personnel are not sufficiently emphasized by many prison administrators
    B. every prison employee is basically an administrator
    C. one inefficient officer can sometimes seriously impair the functioning of an entire institution
    D. the chainlike organization of prison management becomes apparent when a weak officer fails to perform his job properly

14.__

15. The industrial farm is the best type of institution yet developed for the majority of jail prisoners.
Of the following, the BEST justification for this statement is that in an institution of this type

    A. strictest application of advanced classification procedure is possible
    B. the products of inmate labor in large measure pay for the cost of running the institution

15.__

C. there is likely to be freedom from political interference because it is located away from urban centers
D. worthwhile employment and training in desirable surroundings can be afforded every inmate

16. Several studies have shown that the majority of sentenced workhouse prisoners are recidivists.
Of the following, the MOST valid inference based on the preceding statement is that

   A. commitment procedures for certain classes of prisoners should be re-studied
   B. for many prisoners custody, rather than rehabilitation, should be emphasized
   C. the rate of recidivism is greatest among workhouse prisoners
   D. while prison administrators give more attention to rehabilitative measures today, results are generally poor

16.____

17. It is desirable that the prisoners be well-acquainted with the practices and procedures of the parole board. Of the following, the BEST argument in favor of this policy is that

   A. parole practices and procedures often change with a change in the make-up of the parole board
   B. prisoner participation in the formulation of parole board practices and procedures is desirable
   C. prisoners will be less prone to think they were unjustly treated by the parole board
   D. the parole board will be less subject to public criticism

17.____

18. Of the following, the MOST probable reason why public criticism of recreational programs for prisoners is much less common today than it was twenty-five years ago is that the general public nowadays

   A. accepts the rehabilitative objectives of correctional institutions more readily
   B. comprehends the real value of recreation in the correctional program
   C. is more interested in recreation and sports
   D. understands the problems involved in the maintenance of prison discipline

18.____

19. Of the following, the CHIEF value of the indeterminate sentence is that

   A. better discipline is obtained from the prisoner during the period of his incarceration
   B. the length of time to be served can be adjusted to the seriousness of the crime
   C. the sentencing power of the courts is curtailed
   D. the time spent in jail can be related to the rate of rehabilitative progress

19.____

20. Suppose that a study of prison inmates shows that a relatively small percentage of first offenders become second offenders, but that a very large percentage of second offenders commit subsequent offenses.
Of the following, the LEAST valid inference based on the study described is that

   A. correctional procedures presently employed with second offenders are largely ineffective
   B. first offenders offer the most fertile field for rehabilitative efforts
   C. in a random sampling of prisoners, most of those sampled will have committed two or more offenses
   D. it is more difficult to attain success in the rehabilitation of second offenders than in the rehabilitation of first offenders

20.____

21. Progressive penologists GENERALLY are of the opinion that

    A. alcoholics should be sentenced to jail for at least six months so that a cure can be effected
    B. alcoholics should receive an indeterminate rather than a definite jail term
    C. chronic alcoholism is a sickness rather than a crime
    D. treatment for chronic alcoholism should be made compulsory

21.___

22. It has been proposed that wider use be made of fines in lieu of imprisonment as a method of punishment for certain offenses.
Of the following, the BEST argument in support of this proposal is that

    A. contact with prison atmosphere is often an effective deterrent to a repetition of the offense
    B. fines are not difficult to collect
    C. fines can be adjusted to the ability of the offender to pay
    D. imprisonment is expensive for the government

22.___

23. Penologists are generally opposed to the use of force as a method of maintaining prison discipline MAINLY because

    A. it is difficult to limit its use to self-defense or the enforcement of lawful commands
    B. it is of doubtful legality
    C. modern escape-proof institutions have reduced the discipline problem to a minimum
    D. resentment of the use of force by inmates may create, rather than correct, discipline problems

23.___

24. Of the following, the MAIN reason why it is so difficult to eradicate the smuggling of narcotics into a prison is that

    A. it is not possible to measure the personal integrity of prison personnel prior to their appointment to the service
    B. so many prison inmates are drug addicts today
    C. there are so many possible ways for the drugs to enter the prison
    D. the supply of available drugs is constantly increasing

24.___

25. Of the following, the LEAST valid argument in favor of having a commissary in a correctional institution is that the commissary

    A. contributes to the maintenance of inmate morale
    B. helps to reduce the institution's food budget
    C. is an important aid in maintaining discipline
    D. provides funds, not otherwise available, to buy recreational equipment for inmates

25.___

26. Of the following, the CHIEF argument in favor of dormitories over cells as a method of housing prison inmates is that dormitories

    A. are cheaper to construct
    B. are easier to clean
    C. make custodial supervision easier
    D. are preferred by inmates

26.___

27. In comparing the Pennsylvania with the Auburn system of penal discipline, it is MOST   27.____
correct to state that in the

    A. Auburn system the prisoners were completely separated from each other except at
meal time
    B. Auburn system the prisoners were not permitted to talk to each other
    C. Pennsylvania system prison visiting was prohibited
    D. Pennsylvania system the prisoners were allowed to mingle with each other only
when at work

28. The proper Fahrenheit temperature which should be maintained in a cell block during the   28.____
winter months is MOST NEARLY

    A. 60°   B. 65°   C. 73°   D. 75°

29. In the ten years from 1970 to 1980, in the nation as a whole, the   29.____

    A. number of major crimes remained constant but the number of lesser offenses
increased markedly
    B. percentage increase in population was greater than the percentage increase in
major crimes
    C. percentage increase in population was smaller than the percentage increase in
major crimes
    D. percentage increase in population equaled the percentage increase in major
crimes

Questions 30-34.

DIRECTIONS: For each book in Column I below, select the author of the book from Column II;
then write the letter preceding the author's name in the space at the right.

COLUMN I   COLUMN II

30. JAILS - CARE AND TREATMENT OF MIS-   A. Barnes, Harry E., and Teeters, Negley,   30.____
DEMEANANT PRISONERS IN THE   K.
UNITED STATES

                                        B. Glueck, Sheldon and Eleanor

31. NEW HORIZONS IN CRIMINOLOGY   31.____
                                        C. Harris, Mary B.

32. PROBATION AND PAROLE   32.____
                                        D. Monahan, Florence

33. THE TRAINING OF PRISON GUARDS IN   33.____
THE STATE OF NEW YORK   E. Pigeon, Helen D.

34. WOMEN IN CRIME   F. Robinson, Louis N.   34.____

                                        G. Wallack, Walter M.

35. A person with a *psychopathic personality* is

    A.   consistently abnormal in his behavior   B.   feebleminded
    C.   insane and has criminal tendencies   D.   psychotic

35.___

36. A person is considered to be of normal intelligence if his IQ or intelligence quotient falls within the range of

    A. 60-80   B. 70-90   C. 80-100   D. 90-110

36.___

37. The term *malingerer* is MOST correctly applied to an inmate who

    A.   bears an officer a grudge for a long time
    B.   is a habitual liar
    C.   pretends to be ill in order to avoid working
    D.   takes a long time to recover from an illness

37.___

38. Members of the uniformed force of the City Department of Correction are designated as peace officers by the

    A.   Administrative Code
    B.   City Charter
    C.   Code of Criminal Procedure
    D.   Penal Law

38.___

39. According to the Penal Law, escape from lawful imprisonment in this state is ALWAYS a

    A.   felony
    B.   felony if the imprisonment was for a felony
    C.   misdemeanor
    D.   misdemeanor if the imprisonment was for a felony

39.___

40. A writ or order by a magistrate, justice, or other competent authority and addressed to an officer requiring him to arrest the person named therein and bring him before the court to be examined regarding the offense with which he is charged.
The preceding definition refers MOST directly to a

    A.   certificate of reasonable doubt
    B.   mandamus
    C.   warrant
    D.   writ of habeas corpus

40.___

41. The MOST accurate of the following statements about the offenses for which prisoners were sentenced to the institutions of the Department last year is that the

    A.   largest number of male commitments was for disorderly conduct whereas the largest number of female commitments was for vagrancy (prostitution)
    B.   largest number of male commitments was for vagrancy whereas the largest number of female commitments was for disorderly conduct
    C.   number of women committed for drug offenses was about 50% of the number of men committed for drug offenses
    D.   second largest number of male commitments was for gambling whereas the second largest number of female commitments was for petit larceny

41.___

42. Of the inmates committed to the Department last year, the average age of the inmates committed to the workhouse as compared to the average age of the inmates committed to the penitentiary was

    A. higher
    B. higher for male commitments but lower for female commitments
    C. lower
    D. neither higher nor lower

42.____

43. Of all the inmates sentenced to the institutions of the Department last year, those who had any education beyond the elementary school constituted between

    A. 15% and 20%
    B. 10% and 15%
    C. 5% and 10%
    D. 0% and 5%

43.____

44. Last year the average rate of recidivism among workhouse and penitentiary inmates (men and women) in the institutions of the Department was

    A. between 50% and 60%
    B. less than 30%
    C. more than 30%, but less than 55%
    D. more than 60%, but less than 75%

44.____

45. In the detention prisons of the Department, persons charged with felonies GENERALLY constitute

    A. about half of the inmate population
    B. a majority of the inmate population
    C. a minority of the inmate population
    D. less of a discipline problem than persons charged with misdemeanors

45.____

46. It is important that the tier officer be notified as soon as possible of any change in an inmate's court status MAINLY because

    A. a change in an inmate's court status may necessitate a change in custodial super-vision
    B. prison records to be of value must be accurate and up-to-date
    C. subordinates should not be able to justify errors of judgment on the grounds of ignorance of the facts
    D. the tier officer, who supervises many inmates, may find it difficult to remember every detail of each inmate's status

46.____

47. The LEAST accurate of the following statements is that a

    A. commitment under an alternate sentence of a fine or a definite term can be made both to the workhouse and to the penitentiary
    B. maximum workhouse definite sentence is for a longer period than a maximum pen-itentiary definite sentence
    C. maximum workhouse indefinite sentence is for a shorter period than a maximum penitentiary indefinite sentence
    D. minimum penitentiary definite sentence is for a longer period than a minimum workhouse definite sentence

47.____

47

48. A *short commitment* is a commitment issued by a magistrate wherein the defendant is   48.___

   A. held for future action in the Magistrates Courts
   B. held for the Court of Special Sessions
   C. held for the Grand Jury
   D. sentenced by the magistrate for the offense committed

49. When the arresting officer calls for an inmate to produce the inmate in court to answer to   49.___
    the charge, it is important that he be informed by the pen officer of any warrants against
    the inmate MAINLY because

   A. it may be necessary to produce the warrants in court together with the inmate
   B. the inmate may be released on the original charge
   C. the warrants may be for more serious offenses than the present arrest
   D. this information will help to identify the inmate

50. When a prisoner is committed on a direct admission, the officer at the detention pen is   50.___
    required to note on the back of the commitment the condition of the inmate at the time
    when taken into custody by the Department.
    Of the following, the PRINCIPAL reason why this information is important is that

   A. a comparison can be made at the time of release to see if any improvement has
      been made
   B. drug addicts and alcoholics can be noted and segregated
   C. it may influence the determination as to which institution the inmate is to be trans-
      ferred
   D. subsequent charges that an inmate was mistreated while in the Department's cus-
      tody can be refuted

———

KEY (CORRECT ANSWERS)

1. D	11. C	21. C	31. A	41. A
2. A	12. A	22. D	32. E	42. A
3. B	13. A	23. D	33. G	43. D
4. A	14. C	24. C	34. D	44. C
5. D	15. D	25. B	35. A	45. B
6. D	16. A	26. A	36. D	46. A
7. D	17. C	27. B	37. C	47. B
8. A	18. A	28. B	38. C	48. A
9. C	19. D	29. C	39. B	49. B
10. B	20. C	30. F	40. C	50. D

———

EXAMINATION SECTION
TEST 1

DIRECTIONS: Each question or incomplete statement is followed by several suggested answers or completions. Select the one that BEST answers the question or completes the statement. *PRINT THE LETTER OF THE CORRECT ANSWER IN THE SPACE AT THE RIGHT.*

Questions 1-6.

DIRECTIONS: Questions 1 through 6 are to be answered on the basis of the following list of items permitted in cells.

ITEMS PERMITTED IN CELLS	
comb	mop
spoon	towel
cup	letters
envelopes	pen
broom	soap
washcloth	money
writing paper	chair
books	dustpan
toothpaste	brushes
toothbrush	pencil

The questions consist of sets of pictures of four objects labeled A, B, C, and D. Choose the one object that is NOT in the above list of items permitted and mark its letter in the space at the right. Disregard any information you may have about what is or is not permitted in any institution. Base your answers SOLELY on the above list. Mark only one answer for each question.

1.   1.____

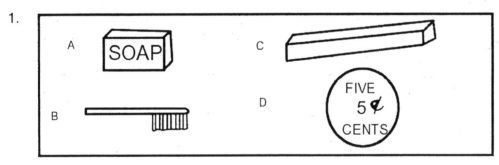

2.   2.____

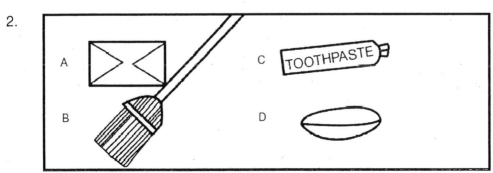

3.

3.___

4.

4.___

5.

5.___

6.

6.___

Questions 7-11.

DIRECTIONS: Questions 7 through 11 are to be answered on the basis of the following list showing the name and number of each of nine inmates.

1	- Johnson	4	- Thompson	7	- Gordon
2	- Smith	5	- Frank	8	- Porter
3	- Edwards	6	- Murray	9	- Lopez

Each question consists of 3 sets of numbers and letters.
Each set should consist of the numbers of three inmates and the first letter of each of their names. The letters should be in the same order as the numbers. In at least two of the three choices, there will be an error.
In the space at the right, mark only that choice in which the letters correspond with the numbers and are in the same order. If all three sets are wrong, mark Choice D in the space at the right.

SAMPLE QUESTION: A. 386 EPM
B. 542 FST
C. 474 LGT

Since 3 corresponds to E for Edwards, 8 corresponds to P for Porter, and 6 corresponds to M for Murray, Choice A is correct and should be entered in the answer space. Choice B is wrong because letters T and S have been reversed. Choice C is wrong because the first number, which is 4, does NOT correspond with the first letter of Choice C, which is L. It should have been T. If Choice A were also wrong, then D would have been the correct answer.

7. A. 382 EGS   B. 461 TMJ   C. 875 PLF   7.____

8. A. 549 FLT   B. 692 MJS   C. 758 GSP   8.____

9. A. 936 LEM   B. 253 FSE   C. 147 JTL   9.____

10. A. 569 PML   B. 716 GJP   C. 842 PTS   10.____

11. A. 356 FEM   B. 198 JPL   C. 637 MEG   11.____

Questions 12-16.

DIRECTIONS: Questions 12 through 16 are to be answered on the basis of the following passage.

Mental disorders are found in a fairly large number of the inmates in correctional institutions. There are no exact figures as to the number of inmates who are mentally disturbed — partly because it is hard to draw a precise line between "mental disturbance" and "normality" — but experts find that somewhere between 15% and 25% of inmates are suffering from disorders that are obvious enough to show up in routine psychiatric examinations. Society has not yet really come to grips with the problem of what to do with mentally disturbed offenders. There is not enough money available to set up treatment programs for all the people identified as mentally disturbed; and there would probably not be enough qualified psychiatric personnel available to run such programs even if they could be set up. Most mentally disturbed *offenders are therefore left to serve out their time in correctional institutions, and the burden of dealing with them falls on correction officers. This means that a correction officer must be sensitive enough to human behavior to know when he is dealing with a person who is not mentally normal, and that the officer must be imaginative enough to be able to sense how an abnormal individual might react under certain circumstances.*

12. According to the above passage, mentally disturbed inmates in correctional institutions   12.___

    A.   are usually transferred to mental hospitals when their condition is noticed
    B.   cannot be told from other inmates because tests cannot distinguish between insane people and normal people
    C.   may constitute as much as 25% of the total inmate population
    D.   should be regarded as no different from all the other inmates

13. The above passage says that today the job of handling mentally disturbed inmates is   13.___
MAINLY up to

    A.   psychiatric personnel   B.   other inmates
    C.   correction officers   D.   administrative officials

14. Of the following, which is a reason given in the above passage for society's failure to pro-   14.___
vide adequate treatment programs for mentally disturbed inmates?

    A.   Law-abiding citizens should not have to pay for fancy treatment programs for citizens.
    B.   A person who breaks the law should not expect society to give him special help.
    C.   It is impossible to tell whether an inmate is mentally disturbed.
    D.   There are not enough trained people to provide the kind of treatment needed.

15. The expression *abnormal individual,* as used in the last sentence of the above passage,   15.___
refers to an individual who is

    A.   of average intelligence   B.   of superior intelligence
    C.   completely normal   D.   mentally disturbed

16. The reader of the above passage would MOST likely agree that   16.___

    A.   correction officers should not expect mentally disturbed persons to behave the same way a normal person would behave
    B.   correction officers should not report infractions
    C.   of the rules committed by mentally disturbed persons
    D.   mentally disturbed persons who break the law should be treated exactly the same way as anyone else
    E.   mentally disturbed persons who have broken the law should not be imprisoned

Questions 17-23.

DIRECTIONS: Questions 17 through 23 are to be answered on the basis of the roster of inmates, the instructions, the table, and the sample question given below.

    Twelve inmates of a correctional institution are divided into three permanent groups in their workshop. They must be present and accounted for in these groups at the beginning of each workday. During the day, the inmates check out of their groups for various activities.

They check back in again when those activities have been completed. Assume that the day is divided into three activity periods.

ROSTER OF INMATES

GROUP X	Ted	Frank	George	Harry
GROUP Y	Jack	Ken	Larry	Mel
GROUP Z	Phil	Bob	Sam	Vic

The following table shows the movements of these inmates from their groups during the day. Assume that all were present and accounted for at the beginning of Period I.

		GROUP X	GROUP Y	GROUP Z
Period I	Check-outs	Ted, Frank	Ken, Larry	Phil
Period II	Check-ins	Frank	Ken, Larry	Phil
	Check-outs	George	Jack, Mel	Bob, Sam, Vic
Period III	Check-ins	George	Mel, Jack	Sam, Bob, Vic
	Check-outs	Frank, Harry	Ken	Vic

<u>SAMPLE QUESTION</u>: At the end of Period II, the inmates remaining in Group X were

    A. Ted, Frank, Harry
    B. Frank, Harry
    C. Ted, George
    D. Frank, Harry, George

During Period I, Ted and Frank were checked out from Group X. During Period II, Frank was checked back in, and George was checked out. Therefore, the members of the group remaining out are Ted and George. The two other members of the group, Frank and Harry, should be present. The correct answer is B.

17. At the end of Period I, the TOTAL number of inmates remaining in their own permanent groups was   17.____

    A. 8   B. 7   C. 6   D. 5

18. At the end of Period I, the inmates remaining in Group Z were   18.____

    A. George and Harry   B. Jack and Mel
    C. Bob, Sam, and Vic   D. Phil

19. At the end of Period II, the inmates remaining in Group Y were   19.____

    A. Ken and Larry   B. Jack, Ken, and Mel
    C. Jack and Ken   D. Ken, Mel, and Larry

20. At the end of Period II, the TOTAL number of inmates remaining in their own permanent groups was   20.____

    A. 8   B. 7   C. 6   D. 5

21. At the end of Period II, the inmates who were NOT present in Group Z were   21.____

    A. Phil, Bob, and Sam   B. Sam, Bob, and Vic
    C. Sam, Vic, and Phil   D. Vic, Phil, and Bob

22. At the end of Period III, the inmates remaining in Group Y were   22.___

   A. Ted, Frank, and George   B. Jack, Mel, and Ken
   C. Jack, Larry, and Mel   D. Frank and Harry

23. At the end of Period III, the TOTAL number of inmates NOT present in their own perma-   23.___
    nent groups was

   A. 4   B. 5   C. 6   D. 7

24. Of the 100 inmates in a certain cellblock, one-half were assigned to clean-up work, and   24.___
    one-fifth were assigned to work in the laundry.
    How many inmates were NOT assigned for clean-up work or laundry work?

   A. 30   B. 40   C. 50   D. 60

25. A certain cellblock has a maximum capacity of 250 inmates. On March 26, there were   25.___
    200 inmates housed in the cellblock. 12 inmates were added on that day, and 17 inmates
    were added on the following day. No inmates left on either day.
    How many more inmates could this cellblock have accommodated on the second day?

   A. 11   B. 16   C. 21   D. 28

KEY (CORRECT ANSWERS)

1. C	11. C		
2. D	12. C		
3. A	13. C		
4. B	14. D		
5. D	15. D		
6. A	16. A		
7. B	17. B		
8. D	18. C		
9. A	19. A		
10. C	20. D		

21. B
22. C
23. B
24. A
25. C

TEST 2

DIRECTIONS: Each question or incomplete statement is followed by several suggested answers or completions. Select the one that BEST answers the question or completes the statement. *PRINT THE LETTER OF THE CORRECT ANSWER IN THE SPACE AT THE RIGHT.*

Questions 1-5.

DIRECTIONS: Questions 1 through 5 are to be answered SOLELY on the basis of the Report of Offense that appears below.

```
┌────────────────────────────────────────────────────────────────────────────┐
│ REPORT OF OFFENSE                              Report No.        26743        │
│                                                Date of Report    10-12        │
│                                                                              │
│ Inmate      Joseph Brown                                                     │
│ Age         27                                        Number     61274        │
│ Sentence        90 days                               Assignment  KU-187      │
│ Place of Offense        R.P.W.  4-1        Date of Offense    10/11           │
│ Offense     Assaulting inmate                                                │
│ Details     During 9:00 p.m. cellblock clean-up, inmate John Jones           │
│             asked for pail being used by Brown.  Brown refused.  Correction   │
│             officer requested that Brown comply.  Brown then threw pail at    │
│             Jones with intent to injure him and said he would "get" Jones.    │
│             Jones not hurt.                                                   │
│                                                                              │
│ Force Used by Officer          None                                          │
│                                                                              │
│ Name of Reporting Officer      R. Rodriguez          No.    C-2056            │
│ Name of Superior Officer       P. Ferguson                                   │
└────────────────────────────────────────────────────────────────────────────┘
```

1. The person who made out this report is   1.____

   A. Joseph Brown   B. John Jones
   C. R. Rodriguez   D. P. Ferguson

2. Disregarding the details, the specific offense reported was   2.____

   A. insulting a fellow inmate
   B. assaulting a fellow inmate
   C. injuring a fellow inmate
   D. disobeying a correction officer

3. The number of the inmate who committed the offense is   3.____

   A. 26743   B. 61274   C. KU-187   D. C-2056

4. The offense took place on   4.____

   A. October 11   B. June 12
   C. December   D. November 13

5. The place where the offense occurred is identified in the report as   5.____

   A. Brown's cell   B. Jones' cell
   C. KU-187   D. R.P.W., 4-1

6. Add $51.79, $29.39, and $8.98.
   The CORRECT answer is

   6.___

   A. $78.97   B. $88.96   C. $89.06   D. $90.16

7. Add $72.07 and $31.54, then subtract $25.75.
   The CORRECT answer is

   7.___

   A. $77.86   B. $82.14   C. $88.96   D. $129.36

8. Start with $82.47, then subtract $25.50, $4.75, and 35¢.
   The CORRECT answer is

   8.___

   A. $30.60   B. $51.87   C. $52.22   D. $65.25

9. Add $19.35 and $37.75, then subtract $9.90 and $19.80.
   The CORRECT answer is

   9.___

   A. $27.40   B. $37.00   C. $37.30   D. $47.20

10. Multiply $38.85 by 2; then subtract $27.90.
    The CORRECT answer is

    10.___

    A. $21.90   B. $48.70   C. $49.80   D. $50.70

11. Add $53.66, $9.27, and $18.75, then divide by 2.
    The CORRECT answer is

    11.___

    A. $35.84   B. $40.34   C. $40.84   D. $41.34

12. Out of 192 inmates in a certain cellblock, 96 are to go on a work detail and another 32 are to report to a vocational class. All the rest are to remain in the cellblock.
    How many inmates should be left on the cellblock?

    12.___

    A. 48   B. 64   C. 86   D. 128

13. Assume that you, as a correction officer, are responsible for seeing that the right number of utensils are counted out for a meal. You need enough utensils for 620 men. One fork and one spoon are needed for each man. In addition, one ladle is needed for each group of 20 men.
    How many utensils will be needed altogether?

    13.___

    A. 1240   B. 1271   C. 1550   D. 1860

14. Assume that you, as a correction officer, are supervising the inmates who are assigned to a dishwashing detail. There is a direct relationship between the amount of time it takes to do all the dishwashing and the number of inmates who are washing dishes. When two inmates are washing dishes, the job takes six hours.
    If there are four inmates washing dishes, how long should the job take?
    _____ hour(s).

    14.___

    A. 1   B. 2   C. 3   D. 4

15. Assume that you, as a correction officer, are in charge of supervising the laundry sorting and counting. You expect that on a certain day there will be nearly 7,000 items to be sorted and counted.
If one inmate can sort and count 500 items in an hour, how many inmates are needed to sort all 7,000 items in one hour?

    A. 2   B. 5   C. 7   D. 14

15.____

16. A carpentry course is being given for inmates who want to learn a skill. The course will be taught in several different groups. Each group should contain at least 12 but not more than 16 men. The smaller the group, the better, as long as there are at least 12 men per group. If 66 inmates are going to take the course, they should be divided into

    A.   4 groups of 16 men
    B.   4 groups of 13 men and 1 group of 14 men
    C.   3 groups of 13 men and 2 groups of 14 men
    D.   6 groups of 11 men

16.____

Questions 17-21.

DIRECTIONS: Questions 17 through 21 are to be answered on the basis of the Fact Situation and the Report of Inmate Injury form below. The questions ask how the report form should be filled in, based on the information given in the Fact Situation.

FACT SITUATION

Peter Miller is a correction officer assigned to duty in Cellblock A. His superior officer is John Doakes. Miller was on duty at 1:30 P.M. on March 21, 2004, when he heard a scream for help from Cell 12. He hurried to Cell 12 and found inmate Richard Rogers stamping out a flaming book of matches. Inmate John Jones was screaming. It seems that Jones had accidentally set fire to the entire book of matches while lighting a cigarette, and he had burned his left hand. Smoking was permitted at this hour. Miller reported the incident by phone, and Jones was escorted to the dispensary where his hand was treated at 2:00 P.M. by Dr. Albert Lorillo. Dr. Lorillo determined that Jones could return to his cellblock, but that he should be released from work for four days. The doctor scheduled a re-examination for March 22. A routine investigation of the incident was made by James Lopez. Jones confirmed to this officer that the above statement of the situation was correct.

```
┌──────────────────────────────────────────────────────────────────────┐
│                    REPORT OF INMATE INJURY                             │
│ (1)   Name of Inmate _____  (2)  Assignment _____  │
│ (3)   Number _____  (4)  Location _____  │
│ (5)   Nature of Injury _____  (6)  Date _____  │
│ (7)   Details (how, when, where injury was incurred) _____  │
│ ─────────────────────────────────────────────────────────────────────│
│ (8)   Received medical attention:        Date _____    Time _____   │
│ (9)   Treatment _____ │
│ (10)  Disposition ( check one or more):                                │
│          ___ (10-1) Return to housing area    ___ (10-2) Return to duty│
│          ___ (10-3) Work release ___  ___ days ___ (10-4) Re-examine in│
│                                                    ___ days            │
│ (11)  Employing reporting injury _____ │
│ (12)  Employee's supervisor or superior officer _____ │
│ (13)  Medical officer treating injury _____ │
│ (14)  Investigating officer _____ │
│ (15)  Head of institution _____ │
└──────────────────────────────────────────────────────────────────────┘
```

17. Which of the following should be entered in Item 1?

   A. Peter Miller　　B. John Doakes
   C. Richard Rogers　D. John Jones

18. Which of the following should be entered in Item 11?

   A. Peter Miller　　B. James Lopez
   C. Richard Rogers　D. John Jones

19. Which of the following should be entered in Item 8?

   A. 2/21/04, 1:30 P.M.　B. 2/21/04, 2:00 P.M.
   C. 3/21/04, 1:30 P.M.　D. 3/21/04, 2:00 P.M.

20. For Item 10, which of the following should be checked?

   A. Only 10-4　　　　　B. 10-1 and 10-4
   C. 10-1, 10-3, and 10-4　D. 10-2, 10-3, and 10-4

21. Of the following items, which one CANNOT be filled in on the basis of the information given in the Fact Situation?
   Item _____.

   A. 12　　B. 13　　C. 14　　D. 15

Questions 22-25.

DIRECTIONS: Questions 22 through 25 are to be answered on the basis of the chart which appears on the following page. The chart shows an 8-hour schedule for 4 groups of inmates. The numbers across the top of the chart stand for hours of the day: the hour beginning at 8:00, the hour beginning at 9:00, and so forth. The exact number of men in each group is given at the lefthand side of the chart. An hour when the men in a particular group are scheduled to be OUT of their cellblock is marked with an X.

	8	9	10	11	12	1	2	3
GROUP Q 44 men	X		X			X		
GROUP R 60 men	X		X	X		X	X	
GROUP S 24 men	X				X			
GROUP T 28 men	X		X		X			

22. How many of the men were in their cellblock from 11:00 to 12:00?   22.____

    A. 60   B. 96   C. 104   D. 156

23. At 10:45, how many of the men were NOT in their cellblock?   23.____

    A. 24   B. 60   C. 96   D. 132

24. At 12:30, what proportion of the men were NOT in their cellblock?   24.____

    A. 1/4   B. 1/3   C. 1/2   D. 2/3

25. During the period covered in the chart, what percentage of the time did the men in Group S spend in their cellblock?   25.____

    A. 60%   B. 65%   C. 70%   D. 75%

KEY (CORRECT ANSWERS)

1.	C		11.	C
2.	B		12.	B
3.	B		13.	B
4.	A		14.	C
5.	D		15.	D
6.	D		16.	B
7.	A		17.	D
8.	B		18.	A
9.	A		19.	D
10.	C		20.	C

21.	D
22.	B
23.	D
24.	B
25.	D

EXAMINATION SECTION
TEST 1

DIRECTIONS: Each question or incomplete statement is followed by several suggested answers or completions. Select the one that BEST answers the question or completes the statement. *PRINT THE LETTER OF THE CORRECT ANSWER IN THE SPACE AT THE RIGHT.*

Questions 1-25.

DIRECTIONS: Questions 1 through 25 describe situations which might occur in a correctional institution. The institution houses its inmates in cells divided into groups called cellblocks. In answering the questions, assume that you are a correction officer.

1. *Correction officers are often required to search inmates and the various areas of the correctional institution for any items which may be considered dangerous or which are not permitted. In making a routine search, officers should not neglect to examine an item just because it is usually regarded as a permitted item. For instance, some innocent-looking object can be converted into a weapon by sharpening one of its parts or replacing a part with a sharpened or pointed blade.*

    Which of the following objects could MOST easily be converted into a weapon in this way? A

    A. ballpoint pen   B. pad of paper
    C. crayon   D. handkerchief

1.____

2. *Only authorized employees are permitted to handle keys. Under no circumstances should an inmate be permitted to use door keys. When not in use, all keys are to be deposited with the security officer.*

    Which one of the following actions does NOT violate these regulations?

    A. A correction officer has given a trusted inmate the key to a supply room and sends the inmate to bring back a specific item from that room.
    B. A priest comes to make authorized visits to inmates. The correction officer is very busy, so he gives the priest the keys needed to reach certain groups of cells.
    C. An inmate has a pass to go to the library. A cellblock officer examines the pass, then unlocks the door and lets the inmate through.
    D. At the end of the day, a correction officer puts his keys in the pocket of his street clothes and takes them home with him.

2.____

3. *Decisions about handcuffing or restraining inmates are often up to the correction officers involved. However, an officer is legally responsible for exercising good judgment and for taking necessary precautions to prevent harm both to the inmate involved and to others.*

    In which one of the following situations is handcuffing or other physical restraint MOST likely to be needed?

3.____

61

A. An inmate seems to have lost control of his senses and is banging his fists repeatedly against the bars of his cell.
B. During the past two weeks, an inmate has deliberately tried to start three fights with other inmates.
C. An inmate claims to be sick and refuses to leave his cell for a scheduled meal.
D. During the night, an inmate begins to shout and sing, disturbing the sleep of other inmates.

4. *Some utensils that are ordinarily used in a kitchen can also serve as dangerous weapons – for instance, vegetable parers, meat saws, skewers, and icepicks. These should be classified as extremely hazardous.*

The MOST sensible way of solving the problems caused by the use of these utensils in a correctional institution is to

A. try to run the kitchen without using any of these utensils
B. provide careful supervision of inmates using such utensils in the kitchen
C. assign only trusted inmates to kitchen duty and let them use the tools without regular supervision
D. take no special precautions since inmates are not likely to think of using these commonplace utensils as weapons

5. *Inmates may try to conceal objects that can be used as weapons or as escape devices. Therefore, routine searches of cells or dormitories are necessary for safety and security.*

Of the following, it would probably be MOST effective to schedule routine searches to take place

A. on regular days and always at the same time of day
B. on regular days but at different times of day
C. at frequent but irregular intervals, always at the same time of day
D. at frequent but irregular intervals and at different times of day

6. *One of the purposes of conducting routine searches for forbidden items is to discourage inmates from acquiring such items in the first place. Inmates should soon come to realize that only possessors of these items have reason to fear or resent such searches.*

Inmates are MOST likely to come to this realization if

A. the searching officer leaves every inmate's possessions in a mess to make it clear that a search has taken place
B. the searching officer confiscates something from every cell, though he may later return most of the items
C. other inmates are not told when a forbidden item is found in an inmate's possession
D. all inmates know that possession of a forbidden item will result in punishment

7. Suppose you are a correction officer supervising a work detail of 22 inmates. All 22 checked in at the start of the work period. Making an informal count an hour later, you count only 21 inmates.
What is the FIRST action to take?

4._

5._

6._

7._

A. Count again to make absolutely sure how many inmates are present.
B. Report immediately that an inmate has escaped.
C. Try to figure out where the missing inmate could be.
D. Wait until the end of the work period and then make a formal roll call.

8. *The officer who is making a count at night when inmates are in bed must make sure he sees each man. The rule "see living breathing flesh" must be followed in making accurate counts.*

8.____

Of the following, which is the MOST likely reason for this rule?

A. An inmate may be concealing a weapon in the bed.
B. A bed may be arranged to give the appearance of being occupied even when the inmate is not there.
C. Waking inmates for the count is a good disciplinary measure because it shows them that they are under constant guard.
D. It is important for officers on duty at night to have something to do to keep them busy.

9. *When counting a group of inmates on a work assignment, great care should be taken to insure accuracy. The count method should be adapted to the number of inmates and to the type of location.*

9.____

Suppose that you are supervising 15 inmates working in a kitchen. Most of them are moving about constantly, carrying dishes and equipment from one place to another. In order to make an accurate count, which of the following methods would be MOST suitable under these circumstances?

A. Have the inmates *freeze* where they are whenever you call for a count, even though some of them may be carrying hot pans or heavy stacks of dishes.
B. Have the inmates stop their work and gather in one place whenever it is necessary to make a count.
C. Circulate among the inmates and make an approximate count while they are working.
D. Divide the group into sections according to type of work and assign one inmate in each group to give you the number for this section.

10. *Officers on duty at entrances must exercise the greatest care to prevent movement of unauthorized persons. At vehicle entrances, all vehicles must be inspected and a record kept of their arrival and departure.*

10.____

Assume that, as a correction officer, you have been assigned to duty at a vehicle entrance. Which of the following is probably the BEST method of preventing the movement of unauthorized persons in vehicles?

A. If passenger identifications are checked when vehicle enters, no check is necessary when the vehicle leaves.
B. Passenger identifications should be checked for all vehicles when vehicle enters and when it leaves.

C. Passenger identifications need not be checked when vehicle enters, but should always be checked when vehicle leaves.

D. Except for official vehicles, passenger identifications should be checked when vehicle enters and when it leaves.

11. In making a routine search of an inmate's cell, an officer finds various items. Although there is no immediate danger, he is not sure whether the inmate is permitted to have one of the items.
Of the following, the BEST action for the officer to take is to

A. confiscate the item immediately
B. give the inmate the benefit of the doubt, and let him keep the item
C. consult his rule book or his supervising officer to find out whether the inmate is permitted to have the item
D. leave the item in the inmate's cell, but plan to report him for an infraction of the rules

11.__

12. *It is almost certain that there will be occasional escape attempts or an occasional riot or disturbance that requires immediate emergency action. A well-developed emergency plan for dealing with these events includes not only planning for prevention and control and planning for action during the disturbance, but also planning steps that should be taken when the disturbance is over.*

When a disturbance is ended, which of the following steps should be taken FIRST?

A. Punishing the ringleaders.
B. Giving first aid to inmates or other persons who were injured.
C. Making an institutional count of all inmates.
D. Adopting further security rules to make sure such an incident does not occur again.

12.__

13. *It is often important to make notes about an occurrence that will require a written report or personal testimony.*

Assume that a correction officer has made the following notes for the warden of the institution about a certain occurrence: *10:45 A.M. March 16, 2007. Cellblock A. Robert Brown was attacked by another inmate and knocked to the floor. Brown's head hit the floor hard. He was knocked out. I reported a medical emergency. Dr. Thomas Nunez came and examined Brown. The doctor recommended that Brown be transferred to the infirmary for observation. Brown was taken to the infirmary at 11:15 A.M.*
Which of the following important items of information is MISSING or is INCOMPLETE in these notes? The

A. time that the incident occurred
B. place where the incident occurred
C. names of both inmates involved in the fight
D. name of the doctor who made the medical examination

13.__

14. A correction officer has made the following notes for the warden of his institution about an incident involving an infraction of the rules: *March 29, 2007. Cellblock B-4. Inmates involved were A. Whitman, T. Brach, M. Purlin, M. Verey. Whitman and Brach started the trouble around 7:30 P.M. I called for assistance. Officer Haley and Officer Blair responded. Officer Blair got cut, and blood started running down his face. The bleeding looked very bad. He was taken to the hospital and needed eight stitches.*
Which of the following items of information is MISSING or is INCOMPLETE in these notes?

    A. The time and date of the incident
    B. The place of the incident
    C. Which inmates took part in the incident
    D. What the inmates did that broke the rules

14.____

15. Your supervising officer has instructed you to follow a new system for handling inmate requests. It seems to you that the new system is not going to work very well and that inmates may resent it.
What should you do?

    A. Continue handling requests the old way but do not let your supervising officer know you are doing this.
    B. Continue using the old system until you have a chance to discuss the matter with your supervising officer.
    C. Begin using the new system but plan to discuss the matter with your supervising officer if the system really does not work well.
    D. Begin using the new system but make sure the inmates know that it is not your idea and you do not approve of it.

15.____

16. *Inmates who are prison-wise may know a good many tricks for putting something over. For instance, it is an officer's duty to stop fights among inmates. Therefore, inmates who want to distract the officer's attention from something that is going on in one place may arrange for a phony fight to take place some distance away.*

To avoid being taken in by a trick like this, a correction officer should

    A. ignore any fights that break out among inmates
    B. always make an inspection tour to see what is going on elsewhere before breaking up a fight
    C. be alert for other suspicious activity when there is any disturbance
    D. refuse to report inmates involved in a fight if the fight seems to have been phony

16.____

17. *Copies of the regulations are posted at various locations in the cellblock so that inmates can refer to them.*

Suppose that one of the regulations is changed and the correction officers receive revised copies to post in their cellblocks.
Of the following, the MOST effective way of informing the inmates of the revision is to

    A. let the inmates know that you are taking down the old copies and putting up new ones in their place
    B. post the new copies next to the old ones so that inmates will be able to compare them and learn about the change for themselves

17.____

C.   leave the old copies up until you have had a chance to explain the change to each inmate
D.   post the new copies in place of the old ones and also explain the change orally to the inmates

18. *A fracture is a broken bone. In a simple fracture, the skin is not broken. In a compound fracture, a broken end of the bone pierces the skin. Whenever a fracture is feared, the first thing to do is to prevent motion of the broken part.*

Suppose that an inmate has just tripped on a stairway and twisted his ankle. He says it hurts badly, but you cannot tell what is wrong merely by looking at it.
Of the following, the BEST action to take is to

A.   tell the inmate to stand up and see whether he can walk
B.   move the ankle gently to see whether you can feel any broken ends of bones
C.   tell the inmate to rest a few minutes and promise to return later to see whether his condition has improved
D.   tell the inmate not to move his foot and put in a call for medical assistance

19. *It is part of institutional procedure that at specified times during each 24-hour period all inmates in the institution are counted simultaneously. Each inmate must be counted at a specific place at a specified time. All movement of inmates ceases from the time the count starts until it is finished and cleared as correct.*

Assume that, as a correction officer, you are making such a count when an inmate in your area suddenly remembers he has an important 9 A.M. clinic appointment. You check his clinic pass and find that this is true.
What should you do?

A.   Let him go to the clinic even though he may be counted again there.
B.   Take him off your count and tell him to be sure he is included in the count being made at the clinic.
C.   Keep him in your count and tell him to inform the officer at the clinic that he has already been counted.
D.   Ask him to wait a few minutes until the counting period is over and then let him go to the clinic.

20. *Except in the case of a serious illness or injury (when a doctor should see the inmate immediately), emergency sick calls should be kept to a minimum, and inmates should be encouraged to wait for regular sick-call hours.*

In which of the following cases is an emergency sick call MOST likely to be justified?
A(n)

A.   inmate has had very severe stomach pains for several hours
B.   inmate has cut his hand, and the bleeding has now stopped
C.   inmate's glasses have been broken, and he is nearly blind without them
D.   normally healthy inmate has lost his appetite and does not want to eat

21. *People who have lost their freedom are likely to go through periods of depression or to become extremely resentful or unpleasant. A correction officer can help inmates who are undergoing such periods of depression by respecting their feelings and treating them in a reasonable and tactful manner.*

    Suppose that an inmate reacts violently to a single request made in a normal, routine manner by a correction officer. Of the following, which is likely to be the MOST effective way of handling the situation?

    A. Point out to the inmate that it is his own fault that he is in jail, and he has nobody to blame for his troubles but himself.
    B. Tell the inmate that he is acting childishly and that he had better straighten out.
    C. Tell the inmate in a friendly way that you can see he is feeling down, but that he should comply with your request.
    D. Let the inmate know that you are going to report his behavior unless he changes his attitude.

21.____

22. An inmate tells you, a correction officer, of his concern about the ability of his wife and children to pay for rent and food while he is in the institution.
    Of the following, which is the BEST action to take?

    A. Assure him that his wife and children are getting along fine, although you do not actually know this.
    B. Put him in touch with the social worker or the correction employee who handles such problems.
    C. Offer to lend him money yourself if his family is really in need.
    D. Advise him to forget about his family and start concentrating on his own problems.

22.____

23. *It is particularly important to notice changes in the general pattern of an inmate's behavior. When an inmate who has been generally unpleasant and who has not spoken to an officer unless absolutely necessary becomes very friendly and cooperative, something has happened, and the officer should take steps to make sure what.*

    Of the following possible explanations for this change in behavior, which one is the LEAST likely to be the real cause?

    A. The inmate may be planning some kind of disturbance or escape attempt and is trying to fool the officer.
    B. The inmate may be trying to get on the officer's good side for some reason of his own.
    C. His friendliness and cooperation may indicate a developing mental illness.
    D. He may be overcoming his initial hostile reactions to his imprisonment.

23.____

24. As a correction officer, you have an idea about a new way for handling a certain procedure. Your method would require a minor change in the regulations, but you are sure it would be a real improvement.
    The BEST thing for you to do is to

    A. discuss the idea with your supervising officer, explaining why it would work better than the present method
    B. try your idea on your own cellblock, telling inmates that it is just an experiment and not official

24.____

C. attempt to get officers on other cellblocks to use your methods on a strictly unofficial basis
D. forget the whole thing since it might be too difficult to change the regulations

25. *Correction officers assigned to visiting areas have a dual supervisory function since their responsibilities include receiving persons other than inmates, as well as handling inmates. Here, of all places, it is important for an officer to realize that he is acting as a representative of his institution and that what he is doing is very much like public relations work.*   25.___

Assume that you are a correction officer assigned to duty in a visiting area.
Which of the following ways of carrying out this assignment is MOST likely to result in good public relations? You should

A. treat inmates and visitors sternly because this will let them know that the institution does not put up with any nonsense
B. be friendly to inmates but suspicious of visitors
C. be stern with inmates but polite and tactful with visitors
D. treat both inmates and visitors in a polite but tactful way

---

KEY (CORRECT ANSWERS)

1. A		11. C	
2. C		12. B	
3. A		13. C	
4. B		14. D	
5. D		15. C	
6. D		16. C	
7. A		17. D	
8. B		18. D	
9. B		19. D	
10. B		20. A	

21. C
22. B
23. C
24. A
25. D

TEST 2

DIRECTIONS: Each question or incomplete statement is followed by several suggested answers or completions. Select the one that BEST answers the question or completes the statement. *PRINT THE LETTER OF THE CORRECT ANSWER IN THE SPACE AT THE RIGHT.*

Questions 1-5.

DIRECTIONS: Answer Questions 1 through 5 on the basis of the following passage.

The handling of supplies is an important part of correctional administration. A good deal of planning and organization is involved in purchase, stock control, and issue of bulk supplies to the cell-block. This planning is meaningless, however, if the final link in the chain — the cell-blook officer who is in charge of distributing supplies to the inmates — does not do his job in the proper way. First, when supplies are received, the officer himself should immediately check them or should personally supervise the checking, to make sure the count is correct. Nothing but trouble will result if an officer signs for 200 towels and discovers hours later that he is 20 towels short. Did the 20 towels "disappear," or did they never arrive in the first place? Second, all supplies should be locked up until they are actually distributed. Third, the officer must keep accurate records when supplies are issued. Complaints will be kept to a minimum if the officer makes sure that each inmate has received the supplies to which he is entitled, and if the officer can tell from his records when it is time to reorder to prevent a shortage. Fourth, the officer should either issue the supplies himself or else personally supervise the issuing. It is unfair and unwise to put an inmate in charge of supplies without giving him ade-quate supervision. A small thing like a bar of soap does not mean much to most people, but it means a great deal to the inmate who cannot even shave or wash up unless he receives the soap that is supposed to be issued to him.

1.   Which one of the following jobs is NOT mentioned by the passage as the responsibility of a cellblock officer?

    A.   Purchasing supplies
    B.   Issuing supplies
    C.   Counting supplies when they are delivered to the cellblock
    D.   Keeping accurate records when supplies are issued

1.____

2.   The passage says that supplies should be counted when they are delivered.
Of the following, which is the BEST way of handling this job?

    A.   The cellblock officer can wait until he has some free time and then count them him-self.
    B.   An inmate can start counting them right away, even if the cellblock officer cannot supervise his work.
    C.   The cellblock officer can personally supervise an inmate who counts the supplies when they are delivered.
    D.   Two inmates can count them when they are delivered, supervising each other's work.

2.____

3. The passage gives an example concerning a delivery of 200 towels that turned out to be   3.__
20 towels short.
The example is used to show that

    A. the missing towels were stolen
    B. the missing towels never arrived in the first place
    C. it is impossible to tell what happened to the missing towels because no count was made when they were delivered
    D. it does not matter that the missing towels were not accounted for because it is never possible to keep track of supplies accurately

4. The MAIN reason given by the passage for making a record when supplies are issued is   4.__
that keeping records

    A. will discourage inmates from stealing supplies
    B. is a way of making sure that each inmate receives the supplies to which he is entitled
    C. will show the officer's superiors that he is doing his job in the proper way
    D. will enable the inmates to help themselves to any supplies they need

5. The passage says that it is unfair to put an inmate in charge of supplies without giving   5.__
him adequate supervision.
Which of the following is the MOST likely explanation of why it would be *unfair* to do this?

    A. A privilege should not be given to one inmate unless it is given to all the other inmates too.
    B. It is wrong to make on inmate work when all the others can sit in their cells and do nothing.
    C. The cellblock officer should not be able to get out of doing a job by making an inmate do it for him.
    D. The inmate in charge of supplies could be put under pressure by other inmates to do them *special favors.*

Questions 6-10.

DIRECTIONS: Answer Questions 6 through 10 on the basis of the following passage.

The typical correction official must make predictions about the probable future behavior of his charges in order to make judgments affecting those individuals. In learning to predict behavior, the results of scientific studies of inmate behavior can be of some use. Most studies that have been made show that older men tend to obey rules and regulations better than younger men, and tend to be more reliable in carrying out assigned jobs. Men who had good employment records on the outside also tend to be more reliable than men whose records show haphazard employment or unemployment. Oddly enough, men convicted of crimes of violence are less likely to be troublemakers than men convicted of burglary or other crimes involving stealth. While it might be expected that first offenders would be much less likely to be troublemakers than men with previous convictions, the difference between the two groups is not very great. It must be emphasized, however, that predictions based on a man's background are only likelihoods — they are never certainties. A successful correction officer learns to give some weight to a man's background, but he should rely even more heavily on his own personal judgment of the individual in question. A good officer will develop in time a kind of sixth sense about human beings that is more reliable than any statistical predictions.

6. The passage suggests that knowledge of scientific studies of inmate behavior would PROBABLY help the correction officer to

    6.____

    A. make judgments that affect the inmates in his charge
    B. write reports on all major infractions of the rules
    C. accurately analyze how an inmate's behavior is determined by his background
    D. change the personalities of the individuals in his charge

7. According to the information in the passage, which one of the following groups of inmates would tend to be MOST reliable in carrying out assigned jobs?

    7.____

    A. Older men with haphazard employment records
    B. Older men with regular employment records
    C. Younger men with haphazard employment records
    D. Younger men with regular employment records

8. According to the information in the passage, which of the following are MOST likely to be troublemakers?

    8.____

    A. Older men convicted of crimes of violence
    B. Younger men convicted of crimes of violence
    C. Younger men convicted of crimes involving stealth
    D. First offenders convicted of crimes of violence

9. The passage indicates that information about a man's background is

    9.____

    A. a sure way of predicting his future behavior
    B. of no use at all in predicting his future behavior
    C. more useful in predicting behavior than a correction officer's expert judgment
    D. less reliable in predicting behavior than a correction officer's expert judgment

10. The passage names two groups of inmates whose behavior might be expected to be quite different, but who in fact behave only slightly differently.
These two groups are

    10.____

    A. older men and younger men
    B. first offenders and men with previous convictions
    C. men with good employment records and men with records of haphazard employment or unemployment
    D. men who obey the rules and men who do not

Questions 11-17.

DIRECTIONS: Questions 11 through 17 are based on the following pictures of objects found in Cells A, B, C, and D in a correctional institution.

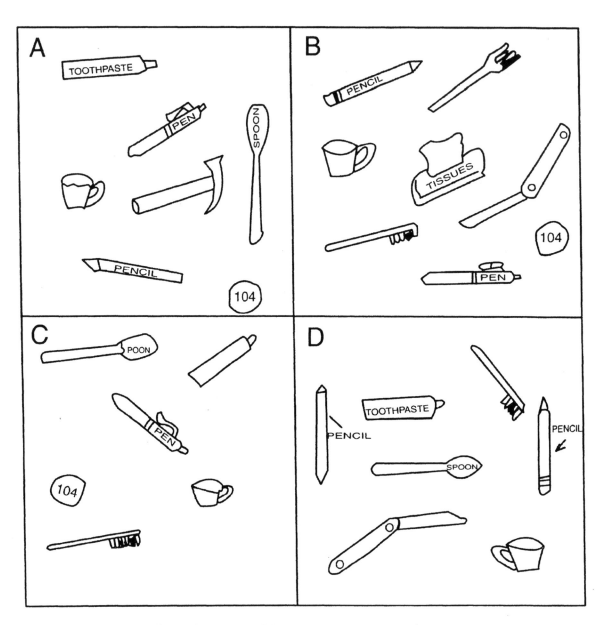

11. Which item can be found in every cell?   11.__

    A. Cup   B. Money   C. Pencil   D. Toothpaste

12. Which cell has toothpaste but no toothbrush?   12.__

    A. A   B. B   C. C   D. D

13. If knives and forks are prohibited in cells, how many cells are in violation of this rule?   13.__

    A. 1   B. 2   C. 3   D. 4

14. One inmate failed to return his tool in the woodworking shop before returning to his cell.   14.__
    That inmate is in Cell

    A. A   B. B   C. C   D. D

15. The cell with the GREATEST number of objects is   15.____

    A. A   B. B   C. C   D. D

16. How many cells have AT LEAST one eating utensil?   16.____

    A. 1   B. 2   C. 3   D. 4

17. Which cells contain money?   17.____

    A. A, B, and C   B. A, B, and D
    C. A, C, and D   D. B, C, and D

Questions 18-22.

DIRECTIONS: Answer Questions 18 through 22 on the basis of the following passage.

A large proportion of the people who are behind bars are not convicted criminals but people who have been arrested and are being held until their trial in court. Experts have often pointed out that this detention system does not operate fairly. For instance, a person who can afford to pay bail usually will not get looked up. The theory of the bail system is that the person will make sure to show up in court when he is supposed to since he knows that otherwise he will forfeit his bail -- he will lose the money he put up. Sometimes a person Who can show that he is a stable citizen with a job and a family will be released on "personal recognizance" (without bail). The result is that the well-to-do, the employed, and the family men can often avoid the detention system. The people who do wind up in detention tend to be the poor, the unemployed, the single, and the young.

18. According to the above passage, people who are put behind bars   18.____

    A. are almost always dangerous criminals
    B. include many innocent people who have been arrested by mistake
    C. are often people who have been arrested but have not yet come to trial
    D. are all poor people who tend to be young and single

19. The passage says that the detention system works *unfairly* against people who are   19.____

    A. rich   B. married   C. old   D. unemployed

20. The passage uses the expression *forfeit his bail*. Even if you have not seen the word *forfeit* before, you could figure out from the way it is used in the passage that *forfeiting* probably means _____ something.   20.____

    A. losing track of   B. giving up
    C. finding   D. avoiding

21. When someone is released on *personal recognizance,* this means that   21.____

    A. the judge knows that he is innocent
    B. he does not have to show up for a trial
    C. he has a record of previous convictions
    D. he does not have to pay bail

22. Suppose that two men were booked on the same charge at the same time, and that the same bail was set for both of them. One man was able to put up bail, and he was released. The second man was not able to put up bail, and he was held in detention. The reader of the passage would MOST likely feel that this result is 22.___

    A. *unfair,* because it does not have any relation to guilt or innocence
    B. *unfair,* because the first man deserves severe punishment
    C. *fair,* because the first man is obviously innocent
    D. *fair,* because the law should be tougher on poor people than on rich people

23. A certain cellblock has 240 inmates. From 8 A.M. to 9 A.M. on March 25, 120 inmates were assigned to cleanup work, and 25 inmates were sent for physical examinations. All the others remained in their cells. 23.___
    How many inmates should have been in their cells during this hour?

    A. 65   B. 85   C. 95   D. 105

24. There were 254 inmates in a certain cellblock at the beginning of the day. At 9:30 A.M., 12 inmates were checked out to the dispensary. At 10:00 A.M.,113 inmates were checked out to work details. At 10:30 A.M., 3 inmates were checked out to another cell-block. 24.___
    How many inmates were present in this cellblock at 10:45 A.M. if none of the inmates who were checked out had returned?

    A. 116   B. 126   C. 136   D. 226

25. There were 242 inmates in a certain cellblock at the beginning of the day. At 9:00 A.M., 116 inmates were checked out to a recreational program. At 9:15 A.M., 36 inmates were checked out to an educational program. At 9:30, 78 inmates were checked out on a work detail. By 10:15, the only inmates who had returned were 115 inmates who had been checked back in from the recreational program. A count made at 10:15 should show that the number of inmates present in the cellblock is 25.___

    A. 127   B. 128   C. 135   D. 137

KEY (CORRECT ANSWERS)

1.	A		11.	A
2.	C		12.	A
3.	C		13.	B
4.	B		14.	A
5.	D		15.	B
6.	A		16.	D
7.	B		17.	A
8.	C		18.	C
9.	D		19.	D
10.	B		20.	B

21.	D
22.	A
23.	C
24.	B
25.	A

———

EXAMINATION SECTION
TEST 1

DIRECTIONS: Each question or incomplete statement is followed by several suggested answers or completions. Select the one that BEST answers the question or completes the statement. *PRINT THE LETTER OF THE CORRECT ANSWER IN THE SPACE AT THE RIGHT.*

1. Of the following, the MOST important reason why a correction officer should always try to maintain a neat appearance while on duty is that   1.____

    A. it is just as easy to be neat as it is to be *sloppy*
    B. it will help her to command the respect and obedience of the inmates she super-vises
    C. she will set an example to young girls who someday may choose this occupation as a career
    D. the overall cleanliness of the prison will be evident when the institution is inspected

2. The one of the following personal traits which it is MOST important for a correction officer in a women's prison to have is   2.____

    A. a complete lack of fear
    B. a high standard of personal honesty
    C. outstanding physical development
    D. superior intelligence

3. In order to maintain good discipline among the inmates under your supervision, you should   3.____

    A. establish a personal and friendly relationship with each inmate
    B. immediately punish an inmate for any infraction of the rules
    C. not permit an inmate to remain seated when she is speaking to you
    D. perform your duties in a business-like, firm, and impartial manner

4. A knowledge of a prisoner's background and of the offense for which she is presently committed will be of value to the correction officer MAINLY because such knowledge will help the officer to   4.____

    A. anticipate and understand problems which may arise in the supervision of the inmate
    B. decide whether the inmate should be treated with greater consideration than the average run of inmates
    C. estimate the general intelligence of the inmate
    D. make the best institutional assignment for the inmate

5. The one of the following which will probably contribute MOST to the reform of a female criminal is   5.____

    A. allowing her to have in prison the same privilege that the ordinary citizen on the outside is entitled to
    B. giving her humane and understanding treatment during the period of her imprison-ment
    C. imposing on her the maximum sentence allowable for the crime she committed

D. making her stay in prison an unpleasant experience so that she will hesitate to commit any future crime after her release

6. Suppose that a prisoner refuses to carry out a routine order that you have given her. Of the following, the MOST desirable action for you to take is to 6.____

    A. confine the prisoner to her cell and submit a report on the incident
    B. deprive the prisoner of privileges for a reasonable time
    C. ignore the incident as it is only routine
    D. use force to compel the prisoner to carry out your order

7. Of the following, the BEST action for you to take with respect to an inmate whom you suspect of suicidal tendencies is to 7.____

    A. always keep her under close watch to make sure she hasn't the opportunity or the means with which to commit suicide
    B. assign another inmate to share her cell
    C. confine her to her cell so that she will not have an opportunity to obtain anything with which to commit suicide
    D. have her put in solitary confinement

8. Suppose that you have under your supervision an inmate who cannot get along with the other inmates and is always quarreling with them.
Of the following, the MOST desirable action for you to take with respect to this inmate is to 8.____

    A. explore the subconscious motivation for her behavior
    B. suggest that she be given an assignment where she can work by herself
    C. tell her that she must learn to get along with others in order to be able to live a normal life
    D. tell the other inmates to leave her alone

9. You have taken a group of inmates in to dinner. An inmate who has a record of being a troublemaker is the first one to begin eating. She calls out in a loud voice that the food is not fit to eat.
Of the following, the BEST action for you to take FIRST in this situation is to 9.____

    A. station yourself at the entrance to the dining room and summon your superior
    B. take a sample of the food from the kitchen and ask another inmate to taste it
    C. tell her that if she is trying to make trouble she is not going to get away with it
    D. tell her that she does not have to eat the food if she doesn't like it

10. As a correction officer, the BEST action for you to take with respect to complaints made by inmates is to 10.____

    A. ignore these complaints since it is only natural for prison inmates to complain
    B. investigate all complaints thoroughly
    C. tell the inmates to submit all complaints to your superior officer as it is her responsibility to handle such matters
    D. weigh the merit of each complaint before you take further action

11. An inmate tells you that the prisoner in the cell next to hers has stolen her cosmetics.   11.____
Of the following, the BEST action for you to take FIRST is to

     A.   *ask* the inmate on what she bases her accusation
     B.   *ask* the inmate to put her complaint in writing, including a description of the stolen articles
     C.   *search* the cell of the accused prisoner
     D.   *search* the person of the accused prisoner when she least expects it

12. Suppose that an inmate asks that you take her to the superintendent of the prison, say-   12.____
ing that she has important information to give her. When you ask the inmate to give the information to you, she refuses to do so.
Of the following, the MOST desirable action for you to take is to

     A.   inform the superintendent of the inmate's request
     B.   order the inmate to give you the important information
     C.   refuse the inmate's request as the superintendent cannot be expected to grant private interviews to individual prisoners
     D.   take the inmate to the superintendent immediately

13. An inmate tells you that she is very upset because she has not heard from her husband   13.____
since she was committed. She pleads with you to visit her husband when you are off duty to find out what is the matter.
Of the following, the BEST action for you to take is to

     A.   advise her to ask another inmate who is about to be discharged to visit her husband
     B.   express your sympathy but tell her you are sorry that you will not be able to do her this favor
     C.   refer her to the social service department of the institution which is established to handle such situations
     D.   visit her home when you are off duty as the situation is obviously having a serious effect on the girl's adjustment

14. In a prison for women, the number of visits a sentenced inmate may receive is limited to   14.____
two a month.
Of the following, the BEST reason for not allowing sentenced prisoners to have unlimited visiting privileges is that

     A.   a correction officer would have to be assigned full-time to supervise such visits
     B.   an inmate's opportunities for escape would be greatly increased
     C.   persons who have broken the law should not be allowed unlimited privileges
     D.   unlimited visiting would interfere with the efficient administration of the prison

15. The inmates under your supervision have just finished their supper meal and are locked   15.____
in their cells. A count of the eating utensils shows that a spoon is missing.
The BEST action for you to take FIRST in this situation is to

     A.   have a thorough search made of the dining room
     B.   line up the inmates and warn them of the consequences if they do not produce the spoon in a reasonable time
     C.   make a thorough search of each inmate's cell
     D.   send a report of the incident to the head of the institution

16. While you are on duty in the visiting room, you observe a visitor pass a letter in a sealed   16.____
and stamped envelope to an inmate. This is prohibited by the institution's rules. Of the
following, the BEST action for you to take in this situation is to

    A. confiscate the letter and immediately make a thorough examination of it to detect
the presence of drugs
    B. confiscate the letter and immediately turn it over to your superior, reporting the inci-
dent to her
    C. pretend not to notice the incident but guard the inmate closely in the future so that
you will be able to foil a possible escape attempt
    D. read the letter and if the contents are harmless, allow the inmate to keep it but
warn her that in the future all mail must be sent through the post office

17. Of the following, the BEST reason for NOT allowing inmates of a correctional institution   17.____
for women to have money on their person is that

    A. more expensive uniforms, with pockets, would have to be provided
    B. the inmates might lose the money
    C. the inmates might use the money to gamble
    D. the institution might be subject to suit if the money were stolen

18. In a correctional institution for women, there is a commissary from which the inmates   18.____
may purchase items such as cosmetics, cigarettes, and candy. The amount of purchase
each inmate may make weekly is limited by the institution's rules.
Of the following, the BEST reason for limiting the amount of such purchases is that

    A. an inmate may purchase an excessive amount of such articles to use them for illicit
purposes
    B. an inmate should be required to save money for the time of her release
    C. excessive consumption of such articles might impair an inmate's health
    D. excessive purchases by some inmates will make it impossible for other inmates to
obtain the articles they desire

19. Suppose that after you have been in the job for several years, a new officer is assigned to   19.____
you for training. You should, at the beginning,

    A. assign her responsibility for the supervision of several inmates who do not present
any problems of discipline
    B. let her observe you as you perform the daily routine of your tour
    C. let her take over responsibility for your tour, in application of the principle of *learn-
ing by doing*
    D. thoroughly explain the rules and regulations to her

20. Although many prostitutes steal from their patrons, they are rarely prosecuted for such   20.____
thievery.
Of the following, the MOST probable reason for such lack of prosecution is that

    A. the courts prefer to prosecute for the more serious offense of prostitution
    B. the objects stolen are usually of little value
    C. there are no witnesses to the commission of the crime
    D. the victim usually does not want to cooperate with the police

Questions 21-27.

DIRECTIONS: Each of Questions 21 to 27 begins with a statement. Your answer to each of these questions MUST be based only upon this statement and not on any other information you may have.

21. At any given moment, the number of people coming out of prisons in the United States is substantially as great as the number entering them.
Of the following, the MOST reasonable assumption on the basis of the preceding statement is that

    A. most prisoners in the United States prisons are recidivists
    B. the crime rate in this country is decreasing
    C. the crime rate in this country is increasing
    D. the prison population of this country is constant

21._____

22. The indeterminate sentence usually sets a lower limit for the time to be served, and an upper limit. In some cases, there is a maximum limit, but no minimum; in some, a minimum but no maximum; and in others, neither a maximum nor a minimum, the time to be served being determined by \ the prisoner's conduct and other considerations. In the preceding statement, the one of the following which is NOT given as a characteristic of the indeterminate sentence is that

    A. sometimes the maximum time which must be served is not set at the time of sentence
    B. sometimes the minimum time which must be served is not set at the time of sentence
    C. the exact length of time to be served is fixed at the time of sentence
    D. the length of time to be served may vary with the prisoner's behavior

22._____

23. Overcrowding in a prison makes segregation of prisoners more difficult, complicates the maintenance of order and discipline, and endangers health and morals.
Of the following, the MOST reasonable assumption based on the preceding statement is that

    A. if prisoners are allowed to associate too freely, their health and morals will be endangered
    B. in a prison that is not overcrowded, there will not be any problems of order and discipline
    C. it is undesirable for the inmate population to exceed unduly the intended capacity of a prison
    D. segregation of prisoners is carried on mainly for the purpose of better prison administration

23._____

24. Most non-professional shoplifters are women of comfortable means who could buy the things they steal.
Of the following, the MOST valid conclusion which can be drawn from the preceding statement is that

    A. some well-to-do women are shoplifters
    B. most professional shoplifters are men
    C. few women practice shoplifting as a profession
    D. most shoplifters suffer from a mental ailment rather than from a moral deficiency

24._____

25. Since accomplices and instigators are harder to detect and successfully prosecute than overt perpetrators, most women offenders, therefore, escape punishment.
Of the following, the MOST valid conclusion which can be drawn from the preceding statement is that

    A. judges deal more leniently with female than with male offenders
    B. men who are accomplices or instigators of crimes are easier to detect and prosecute than women
    C. successful prosecution of women offenders depends to a large extent on their successful detection
    D. women are more often accomplices in, rather than actual perpetrators of, criminal acts

25.____

26. Through the juvenile court, the recognition of social responsibility in the delinquent acts of an individual has been established.
The MOST accurate of the following statements on the basis of the preceding statement is that

    A. delinquent behavior is an evidence of an individual's social responsibility
    B. some individuals are responsible for their delinquent acts
    C. the juvenile court is evidence of society's willingness to assume some blame for the anti-social behavior of its younger members
    D. the juvenile court takes into consideration the age, social background, and offense of the individual before deciding upon his punishment

26.____

27. The way to win more offenders to lasting good behavior is to provide treatment to each offender based on an understanding of the causes of his actions and of his emotional needs in the light of modern insight into human nature. Of the following, the MOST valid inference which can be drawn from the preceding statement is that

    A. few offenders are reformed today because they are not led to an understanding of the causes of their criminal actions
    B. individualized attention is required to achieve reform in criminals
    C. penologists have a better understanding of the causes of criminal behavior because of recent developments in the study of human nature
    D. unsolved emotional conflicts frequently result in criminal acts

27.____

Questions 28-33.

DIRECTIONS: Questions 28 to 33 are based on the paragraph given below. Your answers to these questions MUST be based ONLY upon the information contained in this paragraph and not upon any other information you may have. Each of Questions 28 to 33 consists of two statements. Read the paragraph carefully and then mark your answer to each question according to the following scheme:
    A-   Both statements are correct according to the information given in the paragraph.
    B-   Both statements are incorrect according to the information given in the paragraph.
    C-   One statement is correct and one is incorrect according to the information given in the paragraph.
    D-   The correctness or incorrectness of one or both of the statements cannot be determined from the information given in the paragraph.

PARAGRAPH

The twentieth century has opened to women many pursuits from which they were formerly excluded and thus has given them new opportunities for crime. Can we assume that as a result of this development female crime will change its nature and become like masculine crime through losing its masked character? In periods of pronounced social stress, such as war, in which women assume many roles otherwise open only to men, experience indicates that crimes of women against property increase. Can we assume, further, that simultaneously the amount of undiscovered female crime decreases? Further study contradicts the validity of this assumption. Their new roles have not freed women from their traditional ones. They may have become wage earners and household heads, but they have not stopped being the homemakers, the rearers of children, the nurses, or the shoppers. With the burden of their social functions increased, their opportunities for crime have not undergone a process of substitution so much as a process of increase.

28. As women assumed increased social burdens, there was a marked change in the character of their opportunities for crime.
    Although the crimes committed by women have increased, they are still fewer in number than those committed by men.

28.____

29. Male crime is less masked in character than female crime.
    The opportunities of women to commit crimes have increased in the last fifty years.

29.____

30. In wartime, when they have increased employment opportunities, women commit fewer crimes against property.
    When the social equality of women increases, the number of undetected crimes which they commit decreases.

30.____

31. In the period between 1900 and 1968, women did not gain many new opportunities for employment.
    In a family unit, the role of the shopper is traditionally that of the wife rather than that of the husband.

31.____

32. The crime rate increases in periods of social stress, such as war.
    Because women have not wanted to be limited to their traditional roles of homemaker and rearer of children, they have sought social equality with men.

32.____

33. Wartime is a period of great social stress.
    Although in periods of social stress women assume occupations normally open only to men, they are reluctant to leave such occupations when the period of social stress is ended.

33.____

Questions 34-40.

DIRECTIONS: Questions 34 to 40 are based on the section of the rules given below. Your answers to these questions MUST be based ONLY on these rules and NOT upon any other information you may have. These rules are not intended to be an exact copy of the rules of any institution.

SECTION OF RULES

A. *All members of the department shall treat as confidential the official business of the department. An employee shall under no circumstances impart information to anyone relating to the official business of the department, except when she is a witness under oath in a court of law.*

B. When answering a department telephone, an employee shall give the name of the institution to which she is attached, her rank, and full name.

C. Officers shall not give the name of any bondsman or attorney to inmates. The head of the institution shall be notified immediately when an inmate requests an officer for the name of a bondsman or attorney.

D. All inmates awaiting trial shall be advised that they are entitled to one free ten cent telephone call with the city. All other telephone calls must be paid for by the inmate.

E. Officers assigned to the examination of parcels or letters for inmates shall do so with utmost care. Failure to discover contraband shall be presumptive evidence of negligence.

F. F. When an officer is assigned to accompany an inmate to court₃ to the District Attorney's office, or elsewhere, she must handcuff the inmate and must, under no circumstances, visit any places except such as are designated in the document calling for the inmate's presence.

34. Assume that your name is Mary Jones and that you are assigned to the house of detention as a correction officer with shield number 781. When you answer the institution's phone, you should say
34.____

    A. house of detention, Officer Mary Jones
    B. house of detention, Officer Mary Jones, shield number 781
    C. Officer Mary Jones, shield number 781
    D. This is the house of detention, Officer Jones speaking

35. An inmate awaiting trial asks for permission to make a telephone call to New Jersey. You should
35.____

    A. allow her to make the call if she has not made any other free calls
    B. permit her to make the call at her own expense
    C. tell her that only local telephone calls are permitted
    D. tell her that she will have to pay all charges over ten cents

36. An inmate awaiting trial asks you for the name of a lawyer who will not charge a large fee, as she does not have much money.
You should
36.____

    A. bring her request to the attention of the head of the institution
    B. remind her that under the rules inmates are forbidden to ask an officer for the name of an attorney
    C. tell her that you don't know any lawyers who charge low fees
    D. tell her the state will furnish a lawyer without charge

37. You have under your supervision an inmate whose case received a great deal of publicity in the newspapers. One day, a reporter comes to your home to interview you about this prisoner.
You should
37.____

    A. give him only such information as has already appeared in the daily press
    B. give him only such information as you do not consider confidential
    C. tell him that you are prohibited by the rules from discussing the case with him
    D. tell him that you will grant him an interview if he can produce a letter from the Commissioner giving him permission to interview you

38. You are assigned to deliver a prisoner to the hospital prison ward in accordance with a court order. You are given a department car and chauffeur for this purpose. Before you leave, the superintendent of the prison also gives you some important official papers requiring the commissioner's immediate attention for delivery to central office. On the way to the hospital, you will pass central office.
You should stop at central office

    A. and send the chauffeur in with the papers, while you wait in the car with the prisoner
    B. on your way back from the hospital, after you have delivered your prisoner
    C. to deliver the papers, leaving the handcuffed prisoner in the car in charge of the chauffeur
    D. to deliver the papers, taking the handcuffed prisoner with you

38.____

39. According to the rules, if an article of contraband is successfully smuggled into the prison in a package for an inmate, it is

    A. possible that the contraband may have been extremely well concealed
    B. possible that the employee who inspected the package did not realize that the article in question constituted contraband
    C. probable that the employee who inspected the package was careless
    D. sufficient cause to make the employee who inspected the package subject to dismissal

39.____

40. According to the rules,

    A. an employee may testify about official business in court
    B. only a competent court or the District Attorney can order a prisoner to be produced
    C. sentenced inmates are not allowed to make telephone calls out of the institution
    D. while packages for inmates are censored, their personal mail is not

40.____

41. A knowledge of first aid will be of value to a correction officer in her work MAINLY because such knowledge will

    A. enable her to give immediate, temporary treatment in case of accident or sudden illness
    B. give her a thorough understanding of the anatomy and physiology of the human body
    C. help her to determine if an inmate who says she cannot work is really ill or is just faking
    D. make it possible for her to teach the inmates in her charge how to eliminate accidents

41.____

42. In a small wound which is not bleeding, it is desirable to encourage some bleeding by squeezing toward the wound MAINLY because this

    A. helps to form a blood clot
    B. helps to locate the wound exactly for further treatment
    C. washes out some of the germs
    D. will show whether the wound is near an artery or vein

42.____

43. As a dressing to be applied directly over a wound or burn, it is   43.____

    A. *move desirable* to use cotton, rather than gauze, because cotton is cheaper and just as good
    B. *more desirable* to use cotton, rather than gauze, because cotton is more absorbent
    C. *less desirable* to use cotton, rather than gauze, because cotton is not sterile
    D. *less desirable* to use cotton, rather than gauze, because cotton sticks and is hard to remove

44. Water or other liquid should NOT be administered to an unconscious person. The MOST probable reason for this is that   44.____

    A. an unconscious person would probably consume more of the liquid than would be good for him
    B. an untrained person would not know the proper way to administer such liquid to an unconscious person
    C. someone untrained in first aid might administer a liquid that would be harmful
    D. the liquid might enter the windpipe of the unconscious person and strangle him

45. In a case of stomach poisoning, it is most important to clean out the stomach. For this purpose, it is LEAST effective to administer   45.____

    A. lukewarm water   B. milk of magnesia
    C. set a broken bone   D. stop bleeding

46. The PRIMARY purpose of a tourniquet is to   46.____

    A. prevent infection   B. serve as a sling
    C. set a broken bone   D. stop bleeding

47. Aromatic spirits of ammonia should properly be administered to   47.____

    A. a person who has swallowed poison
    B. clean a wound
    C. deaden pain
    D. revive a person who has fainted

48. The pen officer shall make a thorough inspection of the court pens at the beginning of the tour every day.   48.____
In the court pens operated by the department, this thorough inspection is very important MAINLY because the pens are

    A. directly accessible from the street
    B. not escape-proof
    C. not under the supervision of department of correction personnel at all times
    D. very antiquated for the most part compared with other facilities for housing prisoners

49. When opening or closing a mechanically operated cell door, the officer should, after setting the door in motion, stop such motion for a fraction of a second and then complete the movement of the door.
Of the following, the BEST reason for operating a mechanical cell door in the manner described in the statement is that the

    A. door will not function properly unless it is operated in this way
    B. obstructions in the path of the door can be removed in time
    C. officer can observe if the door is operating properly
    D. fast inmate is warned to get in or out of the cell immediately

49.____

50. Detention prisons house mainly prisoners awaiting trial. A house gang of sentenced inmates is often transferred to a detention prison to do maintenance work throughout the institution.
Of the following, the GREATEST potential danger from such a house gang is that its members will

    A. gain control over inmates awaiting trial by claiming to be *in the know*
    B. have too many opportunities for escape
    C. pass contraband to inmates awaiting trial
    D. upset prison discipline by fighting with inmates awaiting trial

50.____

KEY (CORRECT ANSWERS)

1. B	11. A	21. D	31. C	41. A
2. B	12. A	22. C	32. D	42. C
3. D	13. C	23. C	33. D	43. D
4. A	14. D	24. A	34. A	44. D
5. B	15. A	25. D	35. B	45. B
6. A	16. B	26. C	36. A	46. D
7. A	17. C	27. B	37. C	47. D
8. B	18. A	28. D	38. B	48. C
9. A	19. B	29. A	39. C	49. B
10. D	20. D	30. B	40. A	50. C

READING COMPREHENSION
UNDERSTANDING AND INTERPRETING WRITTEN MATERIAL
EXAMINATION SECTION
TEST 1

DIRECTIONS: Each question or incomplete statement is followed by several suggested answers or completions. Select the one that BEST answers the question or completes the statement. *PRINT THE LETTER OF THE CORRECT ANSWER IN THE SPACE AT THE RIGHT.*

Questions 1-6.

DIRECTIONS: Questions 1 through 6 are to be answered SOLELY on the basis of the following passage.

Delinquency and crime and reactions to them are social products and are socially defined. Society as a whole, not individuals, creates and defines rules, pejoratively labels those who break rules, and prescribes ways for reacting to the labeled person. Moreover, at times the societal process of defining, labeling, and reacting may not affect behavior but at other times it is influential in determining both who shall enter the correctional process and what its outcome will be

What's more, the labeling process is often a means of isolating offenders from, rather than integrating them in, effective participation in such major societal institutions as schools, businesses, unions, and political, community, and fraternal organizations. These institutions are the major access routes to a successful, non-delinquent career. Those who are in power in them are the gatekeepers of society and, if offenders and correctional programs are isolated from them, then the personal wishes and characteristics of offenders will have little bearing on whether correctional programs succeed or fail.

1. According to the above passage, the MAJOR determinant of whether an offender will succeed in society is his

    A. self-confidence and general intelligence
    B. degree of participation in the major societal institutions
    C. attitude toward the entire criminal justice system
    D. overall criminal record

1.____

2. The above passage suggests that the isolation of offenders from certain groups within society through the labeling process is

    A. intentional   B. unlawful
    C. beneficial   D. irreversible

2.____

3. Of the following, the MOST appropriate title for the passage is

    A. METHODS OF REFORMING THE ATTITUDES OF SOCIETY
    B. UNJUST JUSTICE
    C. DELINQUENCY AND CRIME
    D. SOCIETY'S REJECTION OF OFFENDERS

3.____

4. According to the passage, delinquency and crime are created by the 4.___

   A. characteristics of offenders
   B. correctional process itself
   C. operations of society
   D. gatekeepers of major institutions

5. Of the following suggested methods of helping offenders adjust to society, the one which 5.___
   the passage would be LEAST likely to favor would be to

   A. establish cooperative relations between correctional programs in cooperation with
      influential members of society
   B. keep the public informed of current developments in the corrections field by con-
      tributing information to local newspapers
   C. create an organizational structure within correctional institutions which, wherever
      practicable, resembles life in society
   D. encourage offenders to maintain close ties with other offenders with whom they
      become friendly while incarcerated

6. According to the passage, the rehabilitation of the offender is MOST likely to be deter- 6.___
   mined by

   A. the individual inmate himself
   B. dynamic reformation programs
   C. society as a whole
   D. the specific correctional institution

Questions 7-10.

DIRECTIONS: Questions 7 through 10 are to be answered SOLELY on the basis of the following paragraph.

Urban crime rates are generally higher than those prevailing in rural areas. This apparent
preponderance of urban crime has been observed by many criminologists both here and
abroad and, although the factual basis for their conclusion that more crime occurs in urban
areas does not lend itself to close measurement, there seems to be sufficient reason to
accept it at face value. But there is an increasing body of evidence accumulating in the United
States indicative that a profound change in these relationships may be in progress. For murder and rape, the rural crime rate of this country now equals the urban rate. As to all homi-
cides, it exceeds the urban crime rate of the New England, Middle Atlantic, and North Central
states, and shows such impressive advances for aggravated assault and robbery as to
greatly reduce the former disparity. Such changes raise the question whether rural crimes,
reacting to new means of transport and consequent interchange of population, which are
urban influences, may not now be in the process of attaining urban crime levels. Certain it is
that crimes against the person have for centuries been relatively more numerous in rural
areas than crimes against property. Hence, the new trend is in a sense an extension of a condition of long standing.

7. According to the above passage, the statement that crime rates are generally higher in 7.__
   urban areas than in rural areas

A. has not been definitely established although there is strong evidence to support such a view
B. is justified but does not necessarily indicate that more crime is actually committed in urban areas
C. has been definitely established despite some contrary evidence submitted by criminologists
D. is not justified since the facts gathered by many criminologists do not lend themselves to close measurement

8. Concerning the present relationship between rural and urban crime rates, it would be MOST correct to state, according to the above passage, that for   8.____

   A. aggravated assault and robbery, the urban rate remained stationary while the rural rate increased
   B. murder and rape, the rural rate equals the urban rate in the Middle Atlantic states
   C. aggravated assault and robbery, the rural rate was formerly lower than the urban rate
   D. murder and rape, the urban rate is less than the rural rate in the North Central states

9. The development of new means of transport, according to the above passage,   9.____

   A. may or may not be an urban influence but it definitely contributed to a rise in rural crime levels
   B. is an urban influence and may or may not contribute to a rise in rural crime levels
   C. may or may not be an urban influence and may or may not contribute to a rise in rural crime levels
   D. is an urban influence and has definitely contributed to a rise in rural crime levels

10. The new trend is BEST defined, according to the above passage, as a tendency for crimes against   10.____

   A. the person to be more numerous in rural areas than they have been in the past in urban areas
   B. property to be less numerous in urban areas than they are in rural areas
   C. the person to be more numerous in rural areas than they have been in the past in rural areas
   D. property to be more numerous in urban areas than they have been in the past in urban areas

Questions 11-15.

DIRECTIONS: Questions 11 through 15 are to be answered SOLELY on the basis of the following paragraph.

If we are to study crime in its widest social setting, we will find a variety of conduct which, although criminal in the legal sense, is not offensive to the moral conscience of a considerable number of persons. Traffic violations, for example, do not brand the offender as guilty of moral offense. In fact, the recipient of a traffic ticket is usually simply the subject of some good-natured joking by his friends. Although there may be indignation among certain groups of citizens against gambling and liquor law violations, these activities are often tolerated, if not openly supported, by the more numerous residents of the community. Indeed, certain social and service clubs regularly conduct gambling games and lotteries for the purpose of raising funds. Some communities regard violations involving the sale of liquor with little concern in order to profit from increased license fees and taxes paid by dealers. The thousand and one forms of political graft and corruption which infest our urban centers only occasionally arouse public condemnation and official action.

11. According to the above paragraph, all types of illegal conduct are   11.____

    A. condemned by all elements of the community
    B. considered a moral offense, although some are tolerated by a few citizens
    C. violations of the law, but some are acceptable to certain elements of the community
    D. found in a social setting which is not punishable by law

12. According to the above paragraph, traffic violations are GENERALLY considered by society as   12.____

    A. crimes requiring the maximum penalty set by the law
    B. more serious than violations of the liquor laws
    C. offenses against the morals of the community
    D. relatively minor offenses requiring minimum punishment

13. According to the above paragraph, a lottery conducted for the purpose of raising funds for a church   13.____

    A. is considered a serious violation of law
    B. may be tolerated by a community which has laws against gambling
    C. may be conducted under special laws demanded by the more numerous residents of a community
    D. arouses indignation in most communities

14. On the basis of the paragraph, the MOST likely reaction in the community to a police raid on a gambling casino would be   14.____

    A. more an attitude of indifference than interest in the raid
    B. general approval of the raid
    C. condemnation of the raid by most people
    D. demand for further action, since this raid is not sufficient to end gambling activities

15. The one of the following which BEST describes the central thought of this paragraph and would be MOST suitable as a title for it is   15.____

    A. CRIME AND THE POLICE
    B. PUBLIC CONDEMNATION OF GRAFT AND CORRUPTION
    C. GAMBLING IS NOT ALWAYS A VICIOUS BUSINESS
    D. PUBLIC ATTITUDE TOWARD LAW VIOLATIONS

Questions 16-18.

DIRECTIONS: Questions 16 through 18 are to be answered SOLELY on the basis of the following paragraphs.

The rise of urban-industrial society has complicated the social arrangements needed to regulate contacts between people. As a consequence, there has been an unprecedented increase in the volume of laws and regulations designed to control individual conduct and to govern the relationship of the individual to others. In a century there has been an eight-fold increase in the crimes for which one may be prosecuted.

For these offenses, the courts have the ultimate responsibility for redressing wrongs and convicting the guilty. The body of legal precepts gives the impression of an abstract and even-handed dispensation of justice. Actually, the personnel of the agencies applying these precepts are faced with the difficulties of fitting abstract principles to highly variable situations emerging from the dynamics of everyday life. It is inevitable that discrepancies should exist between precept and practice.

The legal institutions serve as a framework for the social order by their slowness to respond to the caprices of transitory fad. This valuable contribution exacts a price in terms of the inflexibility of legal institutions in responding to new circumstances. This possibility is promoted by the changes in values and norms of the dynamic larger culture of which the legal precepts are a part.

16. According to the above passage, the increase in the number of laws and regulations during the twentieth century can be attributed to the 16._____

    A.   complexity of modern industrial society
    B.   increased seriousness of offenses committed
    C.   growth of individualism
    D.   anonymity of urban living

17. According to the above passage, which of the following presents a problem to the staff of legal agencies? 17._____

    A.   The need to eliminate the discrepancy between precept and practice
    B.   The necessity to apply abstract legal precepts to rapidly changing conditions
    C.   The responsibility for reducing the number of abstract legal principles
    D.   The responsibility for understanding offenses in terms of the real life situations from which they emerge

18. According to the above passage, it can be concluded that legal institutions affect social institutions by 18._____

    A.   preventing change
    B.   keeping pace with its norms and values
    C.   changing its norms and values
    D.   providing stability

Questions 19-21.

DIRECTIONS: Questions 19 through 21 are to be answered SOLELY on the basis of the following paragraph.

This research lends additional emphasis to the contention that crime, as reported and recorded in the United States, is largely a function of social and cultural factors rather than biological, psychological, or entirely chance of factors. In the absence of significant biological variations or significant differences in basic mental processes on a regional or sectional basis, all other things being equal, one would expect a rather even crime rate from state to state. Since vast differences in crime rates on a sectional basis are found to persist over a period of time, one may hypothesize that subcultural variations of a regional or sectional nature are responsible for these regional or sectional patterns of crime. Even if this hypothesis cannot be accepted due to underreporting of crime, the least that the data may be said to demonstrate is a distinctly sectional variation in reporting and recording practices, indicating great disparities in sectional reactions to various types of human, or more specifically, criminal behavior.

19. According to the above paragraph, sectional crime rates   19.____

    A.   are not affected significantly by entirely chance factors in the absence of psychological factors
    B.   can be affected by biological variations or differences in basic mental processes
    C.   vary little with significant biological factors in the population
    D.   vary significantly in the absence of variable social and cultural factors

20. According to the above paragraph, great differences in the crime pattern and incidence in   20.____
different sections of the United States may be said to be, assuming adequate reporting,

    A.   a function of sectional variations in reporting and recording practices
    B.   based on the specificity of some types of criminal behavior and the lack of a pattern in others
    C.   based primarily on differences in the extent of urbanization of the population
    D.   the result of regional cultural variations that are persistent over a period of time

21. According to the above paragraph, the statement that is MOST acceptable concerning   21.____
the interpretation of crime data distribution by states or regions is that

    A.   a more or less even crime rate from state to state indicates absence of significant biological variations
    B.   consistent patterns of crime incidence are solely attributable to similar cultural and social factors
    C.   failure to report crime that has occurred is indicative of differences in reaction to different types of crimes committed
    D.   uniform reporting practices tend to eliminate sectional disparities in causality of crime

Questions 22-26.

DIRECTIONS: Questions 22 through 26 are to be answered SOLELY on the basis of the following paragraph.

Criminals were once considered sinners who chose to offend against the laws of God and man. They were severely punished for their crimes. Modern criminologists regard society itself as in large part responsible for the crimes committed against it. Poverty, poor living conditions, and inadequate education are all causes of crime. Crime is fundamentally the result of society's failure to provide a decent life for all the people. It is especially common in times

when values are changing, as after a war, or in countries where people of different backgrounds and values are thrown together, as in the United States. Crimes, generally speaking,
are fewer in countries where there is a settled way of life and a traditional respect for law.

22. This passage deals with 22.____

    A. criminals
    B. society
    C. the reasons for crime
    D. crime in the United States

23. The MAIN idea of this passage is that 23.____

    A. crime is common when values are changing
    B. crime is the result of poverty
    C. traditional respect for law prevents a crime
    D. society is largely responsible for crime

24. According to the passage, which is NOT a cause of crime? 24.____

    A. Poverty   B. Wickedness
    C. Ethnic mixing   D. Unsettled way of life

25. Crime is MOST common in 25.____

    A. periods of instability   B. the United States
    C. wartime   D. suburbs

26. To prevent crime, the author implies that society should 26.____

    A. provide stiffer penalties for criminals
    B. provide a decent way of life for everyone
    C. segregate the poor
    D. give broader powers to the police

Questions 27-30.

DIRECTIONS: Questions 27 through 30 are to be answered SOLELY on the basis of the following passage.

    Perpetrators of crimes are often described by witnesses or victims in terms of salient
facial features. The Bertillon System of identification which preceded the widespread use of
fingerprints was based on body measurements. Recently, there have been developments in
the quantification of procedures used in the classification and comparison of facial characteristics. Devices are now available which enable a trained operator, with the aid of a witness, to
form a composite picture of a suspect's face and to translate that composite into a numerical
code. Further developments in this area are possible, using computers to develop efficient
sequences of questions so that witnesses may quickly arrive at the proper description.

    Recent studies of voice analysis and synthesis, originally motivated by problems of effi-
cient telephone transmission, have led to the development of the audio-frequency profile or
voice print. Each voice print may be sufficiently unique to permit development of a classification system that will make possible positive identification of the source of a voice print. This
method of identification, using an expert to identify the voice patterns, has been introduced in

more than 40 cases by 15 different police departments. As with all identification systems that rely on experts to perform the identification, controlled laboratory tests are needed to establish with care the relative frequency of errors of omission and commission made by experts.

27. The MOST appropriate title for the above passage is   27.____

    A. TECHNOLOGY IN MODERN INVESTIGATIVE DETECTION
    B. IDENTIFICATION BY PHYSICAL FEATURES
    C. VERIFICATION OF IDENTIFICATIONS BY EXPERTS
    D. THE USE OF ELECTRONIC IDENTIFICATION TECHNIQUES

28. According to the above passage, computers may be used in conjunction with which of   28.____
the following identification techniques?

    A. Fingerprints   B. Bertillon System
    C. Voice prints   D. Composite Facial Pictures

29. According to the above passage, the ability to identify individuals based on facial charac-   29.____
teristics has improved as a result of

    A. an increase in the number of facial types which can be shown to witnesses
    B. information which is derived from other body measurements
    C. coded classification and comparison techniques
    D. greater reliance upon experts to make the identifications

30. According to the above passage, it is CORRECT to state that audio-frequency profiles or   30.____
voice prints

    A. have been decisive in many prosecutions
    B. reduce the number of errors made by experts
    C. developed as a result of problems in telephonic communications
    D. are unlikely to result in positive identifications

KEY (CORRECT ANSWERS)

1.	B		16.	A
2.	A		17.	B
3.	D		18.	D
4.	C		19.	D
5.	D		20.	D
6.	C		21.	C
7.	B		22.	C
8.	C		23.	A
9.	D		24.	B
10.	C		25.	A
11.	C		26.	B
12.	D		27.	B
13.	B		28.	D
14.	A		29.	C
15.	D		30.	C

———

TEST 2

DIRECTIONS: Each question or incomplete statement is followed by several suggested answers or completions. Select the one that BEST answers the question or completes the statement. *PRINT THE LETTER OF THE CORRECT ANSWER IN THE SPACE AT THE RIGHT.*

Questions 1-7.

DIRECTIONS: Questions 1 through 7 are to be answered SOLELY on the basis of the following rules. These rules are not intended to be an exact copy of the rules of any institution.

SECTION OF RULES

All members of the department shall treat as confidential the official business of the department. An employee shall under no circumstances impart information to anyone relating to the official business of the department, except when she is a witness under oath in a court of law. When answering a department telephone, an employee shall give the name of the institution to which she is attached, her rank, and full name. Officers shall not give the name of any bondsman or attorney to inmates. The head of the institution shall be notified immediately when an inmate requests an officer for the name of a bondsman or attorney. All inmates awaiting trial shall be advised that they are entitled to one free twenty-five cent telephone call within the city. All other telephone calls must be paid for by the inmate. Officers assigned to the examination of parcels or letters for inmates shall do so with utmost care. Failure to discover contraband shall be presumptive evidence of negligence. When an officer is assigned to accompany an inmate to court, to the District Attorney's office, or elsewhere, she must handcuff the inmate and must, under no circumstances, visit any places except such as are designated in the document calling for the inmate's presence.

1. Assume that Mary Jones is assigned to the House of Detention as a Correction Officer   1.___
    with shield number 781.
    When she answers the institution's phone, she should say

    A.   House of Detention, Officer Mary Jones
    B.   House of Detention, Officer Mary Jones, shield number 781
    C.   Officer Mary Jones, shield number 781
    D.   This is the House of Detention, Officer Jones speaking

2. An inmate awaiting trial asks for permission to make a telephone call to New Jersey.   2.___
    She should be

    A.   allowed to make the call if she has not made any other free calls
    B.   permitted to make the call at her own expense
    C.   told that only local telephone calls are permitted
    D.   told that she will have to pay all charges over twenty-five cents

3. An inmate awaiting trial asks you for the name of a lawyer who will not charge a large fee,   3.___
    as she does not have much money.
    You should

    A.   bring her request to the attention of the head of the institution
    B.   remind her that under the rules inmates are forbidden to ask an officer for the name of an attorney
    C.   tell her that you don't know any lawyers who charge low fees
    D.   tell her the state will furnish a lawyer without charge

4.   A supervisor has an inmate whose case received a great deal of publicity in the newspapers. One day a reporter comes to the supervisor's home to interview him about this prisoner.
   The supervisor should

    A.   give him only such information as has already appeared in the daily press
    B.   give him only such information which is not considered confidential
    C.   tell him that he is prohibited by the rules from discussing the case with him
    D.   tell him that an interview will be granted if he can produce a letter from the Commissioner giving him permission for the interview

4.____

5.   An officer is assigned to deliver a prisoner to the hospital prison ward in accordance with a court order. He is given a department car and chauffeur for this purpose. Before he leaves, the Superintendent of the prison also gives him some important official papers requiring the Commissioner's immediate attention for delivery to Central Office. On the way to the hospital, he will pass Central Office.
   He should stop at Central Office

    A.   and send the chauffeur in with the papers while he waits in the car with the prisoner
    B.   on his way back from the hospital, after he has delivered his prisoner
    C.   to deliver the papers, leaving the handcuffed prisoner in the car in charge of the chauffeur
    D.   to deliver the papers, taking the handcuffed prisoner with him

5.____

6.   According to the rules, if an article of contraband is successfully smuggled into the prison in a package for an inmate, it is

    A.   possible that the contraband may have been extremely well concealed
    B.   possible that the employee who inspected the package did not realize that the article in question constituted contraband
    C.   probable that the employee who inspected the package was careless
    D.   sufficient cause to make the employee who inspected the package subject to dismissal

6.____

7.   According to the rules,

    A.   an employee may testify about official business in court
    B.   only a competent court or the District Attorney can order a prisoner to be produced
    C.   sentenced inmates are not allowed to make telephone calls out of the institution
    D.   while packages for inmates are censored, their personal mail is not

7.____

Questions 8-11.

DIRECTIONS: Questions 8 through 11 are to be answered on the basis of the following passage.

Female criminality is very much under-reported, especially if one considers offenses such as shoplifting, thefts by prostitutes, offenses against children, and homicide. There are even certain offenses such as homosexuality and exhibitionism that go practically unprosecuted if committed by women. Female offenders are really protected by men, even by victims, who are usually disinclined to complain to authorities. Since women play much less active roles in society than men do, one must be prepared for the fact that women are often the instigators of crimes committed by men and, as instigators, they are hard to detect. There are several crimes that are ordinarily highly detectable in men but have very low detectability in women. Her roles as homemaker, mother, nurse, wife, and so forth, permit the female to commit a crime and yet screen that crime from public view - for example, slowly poisoning her husband or treating her children abusively. In addition, law enforcement officers, judges, and juries are much more lenient toward women than toward men. Such considerations lead to the conclusion that criminality of women is *largely masked criminality*. Consequently, official statistics and records of criminality should be expected to under-report female offenses. The true measure of female crime must be sought from unofficial sources. The masked character of female crime and its gross under-reporting are consistent with the official view that the female is a very low risk for crime.

8. What has the writer inferred about the incidence of female offenses?   8.____

    A. It gives an adequate representation of the number of crimes committed by men but instigated by women.
    B. It is not to be considered an important area of criminality.
    C. It is understated because the classic female role makes her less visible to social scrutiny.
    D. In every crime the incidence of male offenses is more difficult to detect than that of women.

9. Judges are inclined to be lenient toward female offenders because   9.____

    A. the role of the woman in society has stereotyped her as maternal and non-hostile
    B. the majority of their crimes does not physically harm others
    C. they commit crimes which are difficult to detect
    D. official statistics report them as less likely to commit crimes

10. Of the following, the title MOST suitable for this passage is   10.____

    A. MALE CRIMINALITY
    B. THE PETTY OFFENDER
    C. THE FEMALE MURDERER
    D. EXPOSING FEMALE CRIMINALITY

11. According to the passage, which of the following crimes is LEAST likely to be prosecuted   11.____
against a woman?

    A. Child abuse   B. Exhibitionism
    C. Homicide   D. Prostitution

Questions 12-16.

DIRECTIONS: Questions 12 through 16 are to be answered SOLELY on the basis of the following paragraph. Each of the questions consists of two statements. Read the paragraph carefully, and then mark your answer

      A - if both statements are correct according to the information given in the paragraph

      B - if both statements are incorrect according to the information given in the paragraph

      C - if one statement is correct and one is incorrect according to the information given in the paragraph

      D - if the correctness or incorrectness of one or both of the statements cannot be determined from the information given in the paragraph.

The twentieth century has opened to women many pursuits from which they were formerly excluded and thus has given them new opportunities for crime. Can we assume that as a result of this development female crime will change its nature and become like masculine crime through losing its masked character? In periods of pronounced social stress, such as war, in which women assume many roles otherwise open only to men, experience indicates that crimes of women against property increase. Can we assume, further, that simultaneously the amount of undiscovered female crime decreases? Further study contradicts the validity of this assumption. Their new roles have become wage earners and household heads, but they have not stopped being the homemakers, the rearers of children, the nurses, or the shoppers. With the burden of their social functions increased, their opportunities for crime have not undergone a process of substitution so much as a process of increase.

12.   I. As women assumed increased social burdens, there was a marked change in the character of their opportunities for crime.   12.____

      II. Although the crimes committed by women have increased, they are still fewer in number than those committed by men.

13.   I. Male crime is less masked in character than female crime.   13.____

      II. The opportunities of women to commit crimes have increased in the last fifty years.

14.   I. In wartime, when they have increased employment opportunities, women commit fewer crimes against property.   14.____

      II. When the social equality of women increases, the number of undetected crimes which they commit decreases.

15.   I. In the period between 1900 and 1968, women did not gain many new opportunities for employment.   15.____

      II. In a family unit, the role of the shopper is traditionally that of the wife rather than that of the husband.

16.   I. The crime rate increases in periods of social stress, such as war.   16.____

      II. Because women have not wanted to be limited to their traditional roles of homemaker and rearer of children, they have sought social equality with men.

Questions 17-18.

DIRECTIONS: Questions 17 and 18 are to be answered SOLELY on the basis of the following passage.

The public has become increasingly aware that rehabilitation that great battle cry of prison reform is one of the great myths of 20th century penology. The hard truth is that punishment and retribution are the primary, if not the only, functions served by most correctional institutions. Courts can provide enlightened rule-making to assist prison reform and ombudsmen can give prisoners a forum to consider their complaints but the results would be limited. The corrections system will never run with any real efficiency until: (a) prisoners want to be reformed; (b) prison administrators want to help them reform; (c) courts want to help both toward a system of reform; and (d) they all define reform in the same way. If this is not done, the criminal justice system will continue to operate on the model of concentric layers of coercion, a grossly inefficient model.

17. According to the above passage, all of the following will be required in order to improve the corrections system EXCEPT

    A. commitment to reform by prison administrators
    B. development by penal experts of criteria for meaningful rehabilitation
    C. acceptance by prisoners of the need for their cooperation
    D. assistance by the courts in providing a system where reform is possible

17.____

18. According to the above selection, meaningful prison reform is MOST likely to result from

    A. the appointment of ombudsmen to replace the courts in ruling on prisoners' complaints
    B. coordination by sociologists of efforts to improve prison conditions
    C. a realization by society that rehabilitation of prisoners is no longer a realistic objective
    D. the joint efforts of those directly concerned and a common understanding of the goals to be achieved

18.____

Questions 19-25.

DIRECTIONS: Each of Questions 19 through 25 begins with a statement. Your answer to each of these questions MUST be based only upon this statement and not on any other information you may have.

19. At any given moment, the number of people coming out of prisons in the United States is substantially as great as the number entering them.
Of the following, the MOST reasonable assumption on the basis of the preceding statement is that

    A. most prisoners in the United States prisons are recidivists
    B. the crime rate in this country is decreasing
    C. the crime rate in this country is increasing
    D. the prison population of this country is constant

19.____

20. The indeterminate sentence usually sets a lower limit for the time to be served, and an upper limit. In some cases, there is a maximum limit, but no minimum; in some, a minimum but no maximum; and in others, neither a maximum nor a minimum, the time to be served being determined by the prisoner's conduct and other considerations.
In the preceding statement, the one of the following which is NOT given as a characteristic of the indeterminate sentence is that

    A. sometimes the maximum time which must be served is not set at the time of sentence
    B. sometimes the minimum time which must be served is not set at the time of sentence
    C. the exact length of time to be served is fixed at the time of sentence
    D. the length of time to be served may vary with the prisoner's behavior

20.____

21. Overcrowding in a prison makes segregation of prisoners more difficult, complicates the maintenance of order and discipline, and endangers health and morals.
Of the following, the MOST reasonable assumption based on the preceding statement is that

    A. if prisoners are allowed to associate too freely their health and morals will be endangered
    B. in a prison that is not overcrowded there will not be any problems of order and discipline
    C. it is undesirable for the inmate population to exceed unduly the intended capacity of a prison
    D. segregation of prisoners is carried on mainly for the purpose of better prison administration

21.____

22. Most non-professional shoplifters are women of comfortable means who could buy the things they steal.
Of the following, the MOST valid conclusion which can be drawn from the preceding statement is that

    A. some well-to-do women are shoplifters
    B. most professional shoplifters are men
    C. few women practice shoplifting as a profession
    D. most shoplifters suffer from a mental ailment rather than from a moral deficiency

22.____

23. Since accomplices and instigators are harder to detect and successfully prosecute than overt perpetrators, most women offenders therefore escape punishment.
Of the following, the MOST valid conclusion which can be drawn from the preceding statement is that

    A. judges deal more leniently with female than with male offenders
    B. men who are accomplices or instigators of crimes are easier to detect and prosecute than women
    C. successful prosecution of women offenders depends to a large extent on their successful detection
    D. women are more often accomplices in, rather than actual perpetrators of, criminal acts

23.____

24. Through the juvenile court, the recognition of social responsibility in the delinquent acts   24.____
of an individual has been established.
The MOST accurate of the following statements on the basis of the preceding statement is that

    A.   delinquent behavior is an evidence of an individual's social irresponsibility
    B.   some individuals are responsible for their delinquent acts
    C.   the juvenile court is evidence of society's willingness to assume some blame for the anti-social behavior of its younger members
    D.   the juvenile court takes into consideration the age, social background, and offense of the individual before deciding upon his punishment

25. The way to win more offenders to lasting good behavior is to provide treatment to each   25.____
offender based on an understanding of the causes of his actions and of his emotional needs in the light of modern insight into human nature. Of the following, the MOST valid inference which can be drawn from the preceding statement is that

    A.   few offenders are reformed today because they are not led to an understanding of the causes of their criminal actions
    B.   individualized attention is required to achieve reform in criminals
    C.   penologists have a better understanding of the causes of criminal behavior because of recent developments in the study of human nature
    D.   unsolved emotional conflicts frequently result in criminal acts

---

KEY (CORRECT ANSWERS)

1.	A		11.	B
2.	B		12.	D
3.	A		13.	A
4.	C		14.	B
5.	B		15.	C
6.	C		16.	D
7.	A		17.	B
8.	C		18.	D
9.	A		19.	D
10.	D		20.	C

21.	C
22.	A
23.	D
24.	C
25.	B

READING COMPREHENSION
UNDERSTANDING AND INTERPRETING WRITTEN MATERIAL

EXAMINATION SECTION
TEST 1

DIRECTIONS: Each question or incomplete statement is followed by several suggested answers or completions. Select the one that BEST answers the question or completes the statement. *PRINT THE LETTER OF THE CORRECT ANSWER IN THE SPACE AT THE RIGHT.*

1. Custody in prison work used to be considered of such supreme importance that everything else was secondary. This statement implies MOST directly that   1.____

    A. formerly nothing was as important as custody in prison work
    B. formerly only custody was considered important in prison work
    C. today all aspects of prison work are considered equally important
    D. today reform of the prisoner is considered more important than custody

2. Since the total inmate treatment and training program is conditioned largely by custody requirements, its success is almost wholly dependent on flexibility of custody classification and handling of prisoners.   2.____
Of the following, the MOST accurate statement based on the above statement is that the

    A. conditions of custody are completely dependent on the handling of inmates in accordance with their classification
    B. daily schedule at the institution should be flexible in order for the treatment and training program to succeed
    C. main factor influencing the inmate treatment and training program is the requirement for the proper safekeeping of inmates
    D. most important factor in the success of the treatment and training program is the cooperation of the inmates

3. An officer's revolver is a defensive and not offensive weapon.   3.____
On the basis of this statement only, an officer should BEST draw his revolver to

    A. fire at an unarmed burglar
    B. force a suspect to confess
    C. frighten a juvenile delinquent
    D. protect his own life

4. Prevention of crime is of greater value to the community than the punishment of crime.   4.____
If this statement is accepted as true, GREATEST emphasis should be placed on

    A. malingering   B. medication
    C. imprisonment   D. rehabilitation

5. The criminal is rarely or never reformed. Acceptance of this statement as true would mean that GREATEST emphasis should be placed on   5.____

    A. imprisonment   B. parole
    C. probation   D. malingering

6. Physical punishment of prison inmates has been shown by experience not only to be ineffective but to be dangerous and, in the long run, destructive of good discipline. According to the preceding statement, it is MOST reasonable to assume that, in the supervision of prison inmates,

    6.___

    A.   a good correction officer would not use physical punishment
    B.   it is permissible for a good correction officer to use a limited amount of physical punishment to enforce discipline
    C.   physical punishment improves discipline temporarily
    D.   the danger of public scandal is basic in cases where physical punishment is used

7. There is no clear evidence that criminals, as a group, differ from non-criminals in their basic psychological needs.
On the basis of this statement, it is MOST reasonable to assume that criminals and non-criminals

    7.___

    A.   are alike in some important respects
    B.   are alike in their respective backgrounds
    C.   differ but slightly in all respects
    D.   differ in physical characteristics

8. Neither immediate protection for the community nor long-range reformation of the prisoner can be achieved by prison personnel who express toward the offender whatever feelings of frustration, fear, jealousy, or hunger for power they may have.
Of the following, the CHIEF significance of this statement for correction officers is that, in their daily work, they should

    8.___

    A.   be on the constant lookout for opportunities to prove their courage to inmates
    B.   not allow deeply personal problems to affect their relations with the inmates
    C.   not try to advance themselves on the job because of personal motives
    D.   spend a good part of their time examining their own feelings in order to understand better those of the inmates

9. Since ninety-five percent of prison inmates are released, and a great majority of these within two to three years, a prison which does nothing more than separate the criminal from society offers little promise of real protection to society.
Of the following, the MOST valid reference which may be drawn from the preceding statement is that

    9.___

    A.   once it has been definitely established that a person has criminal tendencies, that person should be separated for the rest of his life from ordinary society
    B.   prison sentences in general are much too short and should be lengthened to afford greater protection to society
    C.   punishment, rather than separation of the criminal from society, should be the major objective of a correctional prison
    D.   when a prison system produces no change in prisoners, and the period of imprisonment is short, the period during which society is protected is also short

10. A great handicap to successful correctional work lies in the negative response of the general community to the offender. Public attitudes of hostility toward, and rejection of, an ex-prisoner can undo the beneficial effects of even an ideal correctional system. Of the following, the CHIEF implication of this statement is that

    A. a friendly community attitude will insure the successful reformation of the ex-prisoner

    B. correctional efforts with most prisoners would generally prove successful if it were not for public hostility toward the former inmate

    C. in the long run, even an ideal correctional system cannot successfully reform criminals

    D. the attitude of the community toward an ex-prisoner is an important factor in determining whether or not an ex-prisoner reforms

10.____

11. While retribution and deterrence as a general philosophy in correction are widely condemned, no one raises any doubt as to the necessity for secure custody of some criminals. Of the following, the MOST valid conclusion based on the preceding statement is that the

    A. gradual change in the philosophy of correction has not affected custody practices

    B. need for safe custody of some criminals is not questioned by anyone

    C. philosophy of retribution, as shown in some correctional systems, has led to wide condemnation of custodial practices applied to all types of criminals

11.____

Questions 12-13.

DIRECTIONS: Questions 12 and 13 are to be answered SOLELY on the basis of the information contained in the following paragraph.

Those correction theorists who are in agreement with severe and rigid controls as a normal part of the correctional process are confronted with a contradiction; this is so because a responsibility which is consistent with freedom cannot be developed in a repressive atmosphere. They do not recognize this contradiction when they carry out their programs with dictatorial force and expect convicted criminals exposed to such programs to be reformed into free and responsible citizens.

12. According to the above paragraph, those correction theorists are faced with a contradiction who

    A. are in favor of the enforcement of strict controls in a prison

    B. believe that to develop a sense of responsibility, freedom must not be restricted

    C. take the position that the development of responsibility consistent with freedom is not possible in a repressive atmosphere

    D. think that freedom and responsibility can be developed only in a democratic atmosphere

12.____

13. According to the above paragraph, a repressive atmosphere in a prison

    A. does not conform to present day ideas of freedom of the individual

    B. is admitted by correction theorists to be in conflict with the basic principles of the normal correctional process

13.____

C. is advocated as the best method of maintaining discipline when rehabilitation is of secondary importance
D. is not suitable for the development of a sense of responsibility consistent with freedom

14. To state the matter in simplest terms, just as surely as some people are inclined to commit crimes, so some people are prevented from committing crimes by the fear of the consequences to themselves.
Of the following, the MOST logical conclusion based on this statement is that   14.___

A. as many people are prevented from committing criminal acts as actually commit criminal acts
B. most men are not inclined to commit crimes
C. people who are inclined to violate the law are usually deterred from their purpose
D. there are people who have a tendency to commit crimes and people who are deterred from crime

15. Probation is a judicial instrument whereby a judge may withhold execution of a sentence upon a convicted person in order to give opportunity for rehabilitation in the community under the guidance of an officer of the court. According to the preceding statement, it is MOST reasonable to assume that   15.___

A. a person on probation must report to the court at least once a month
B. a person who has been convicted of crime is sometimes placed on probation by the judge
C. criminals who have been rehabilitated in the community are placed on probation by the court after they are sentenced
D. the chief purpose of probation is to make the sentence easier to serve

Questions 16-19.

DIRECTIONS: Questions 16 through 19 are to be answered SOLELY on the basis of the following passage.

Traditional correctional institutions do not change or redirect the behavior of many of their inmates. Few of these establishments are equipped with adequate resources to treat the social and psychological handicaps of their wards. Too often, far removed ideologically from the world to which its charges must return, the institution often compounds the problems its corrective mechanisms are intended to cure. Training school academic programs, for example, range from poor to totally inadequate and usually reinforce negative feelings toward future learning experiences. Vocational programs are frequently designed to benefit the institution without regard to the inmate, and the usual low-key common denominator *treatment* program scarcely begins to meet the needs of many offenders.

Most correctional institutions must mobilize their limited resources in time and talent for purposes other than the ever-present concern about runaways or escapes. No one could quarrel rationally with the need to safeguard the community and control the behavior of people who may be of danger to themselves or others. It is ridiculous and tragic, however, that an overstated security approach is still the rule for the bulk of our correctional population.

16. The passage states that inmates of traditional correctional institutions are LIKELY to   16.____
    A. develop belief in radical political ideologies
    B. experience conditions that produce no betterment
    C. give major attention to devising plans of escape
    D. desire vocational training unrelated to their individual potential

17. The passage indicates that traditional training school academic programs lead inmates   17.____
    to
    A. adjust to the institutional setting
    B. avoid later formal learning
    C. develop respect for the values of education
    D. request more practical, vocational training

18. The passage indicates that most traditional correctional institutions, because of their   18.____
    ideological distance from the realities of the outside world, are MOST likely to
    A. ignore the safety of the outside community
    B. favor a minority of the inmate population
    C. lack properly motivated staff
    D. increase the problems of inmates

19. The passage states that the strong custodial function in most correctional institutions is   19.____
    MOST likely to be
    A. accorded excessive emphasis
    B. aimed at incorrigible inmates only
    C. necessary to redirect inmate behavior
    D. resented by the outside community

Questions 20-22.

DIRECTIONS: Questions 20 through 22 are to be answered SOLELY on the basis of the following passage.

The most widely accepted argument in favor of the death penalty is that the threat of its infliction deters people from committing capital offenses. Of course, since human behavior can be influenced through fear, and since man tends to fear death, it is possible to use capital punishment as a deterrent. But the real question is whether individuals think of the death penalty BEFORE they act, and whether they are thereby deterred from committing crimes. If for the moment we assume that the death penalty does this to some extent, we must also grant that certain human traits limit its effectiveness as a deterrent. Man tends to be a creature of habit and emotion, and when he is handicapped by poverty, ignorance, and malnutrition, as criminals often are, he becomes notoriously shortsighted. Many violators of the law give little thought to the possibility of detection and apprehension, and often they do not even consider the penalty. Moreover, it appears that most people do not regulate their lives in terms of the pleasure and pain that may result from their acts.

Human nature is very complex. A criminal may fear punishment, but he may fear the anger and contempt of his companions or his family even more, and the fear of economic insecurity or exclusion from the group whose respect he cherishes may drive him to commit the most daring crimes. Besides, fear is not the only emotion that motivates man. Love, loy-alty, ambition, greed, lust, anger, and resentment may steel him to face even death in the perpetration of crime, and impel him to devise the most ingenious methods to get what he wants and to avoid detection.

If the death penalty were surely, quickly, uniformly, publicly, and painfully inflicted, it undoubtedly would prevent many capital offenses that are being committed by those who do consider the punishment that they may receive for their crimes. But this is precisely the point. Certainly, the way in which the death penalty has been administered in the United States is not fitted to produce this result.

20. Of the following, the MOST appropriate title for the above passage is   20.____

    A.   CAPITAL OFFENSES IN THE UNITED STATES
    B.   THE DEATH PENALTY AS A DETERRENT
    C.   HUMAN NATURE AND FEAR
    D.   EMOTION AS A CAUSE OF CRIME

21. The above passage implies that the death penalty, as it has been administered in the   21.____
United States,

    A.   was too prompt and uniform to be effective
    B.   deterred many criminals who considered the possible consequences of their actions
    C.   prevented crimes primarily among habitual criminals
    D.   failed to prevent the commission of many capital offenses

22. According to the above passage, many violators of the law are   22.____

    A.   intensely concerned with the pleasure or pain that may result from their acts
    B.   influenced primarily by economic factors
    C.   not influenced by the opinions of their family or friends
    D.   not seriously concerned with the possibility of apprehension

Questions 23-25.

DIRECTIONS: Questions 23 through 25 are to be answered SOLELY on the basis of the information contained in the following paragraph.

As a secondary aspect of this revolutionary change in outlook resulting from the introduction of group counseling into the adult correctional institution, there must evolve a new type of prison employee, the true correctional or treatment worker. The top management will have to reorient their attitudes toward subordinate employees, respecting and accepting them as equal participants in the work of the institution. Rank may no longer be the measure of value in the inmate treatment program. Instead, the employee will be valuable whatever his location in the prison hierarchy or administrative plan in terms of his capacity constructively to relate himself to inmates as one human being to another. In group counseling, all employees must consider it their primary task to provide a wholesome environment for personality growth for the inmates in work crews, cell blocks, clerical pools, or classrooms. The above does not mean that custodial care and precautions regarding the prevention of disorders or escapes are cast aside or discarded by prison workers. On the contrary, the staff will be more acutely aware of the costs to the inmates of such infractions of institutional rules. Gradually, it is hoped, these instances of uncontrolled responses to over-powering feelings by inmates will become much less frequent in the treatment institution, In general, men in group counseling provide considerably fewer disciplinary infractions when compared with a control group of those still on a waiting list to enter group counseling, and especially fewer than those who do not choose to participate. It is optimistically anticipated that some day men in prison may have the same attitudes toward the staff, the same security in expecting treatment as do patients in a good general hospital.

23. According to the above paragraph, under a program of group counseling in an adult correctional institution, that employee will be MOST valuable in the inmate treatment program who   23.____

    A. can establish a constructive relationship of one human being to another between himself and the inmate
    B. gets top management to accept him as an equal participant in the work of the institution
    C. is in contact with the inmate in work crews, cell blocks, clerical pools or classrooms
    D. provides the inmate with a proper home environment for wholesome personality growth

24. According to the above paragraph, an effect that the group counseling program is expected to have on the problem of custody and discipline in a prison is that the staff will   24.____

    A. be more acutely aware of the cost of maintaining strict prison discipline
    B. discard old and outmoded notions of custodial care and the prevention of disorders and escapes
    C. neglect this aspect of prison work unless proper safeguards are established
    D. realize more deeply the harmful effect on the inmate of breaches of discipline

25. According to the above paragraph, a result that is expected from the group counseling method of inmate treatment in an adult correctional institution is   25.____

    A. a greater desire on the part of potential delinquents to enter the correctional institution for the purpose of securing treatment
    B. a large reduction in the number of infractions of institutional rules by inmates
    C. a steady decrease in the crime rate
    D. the introduction of hospital methods of organization and operation into the correctional institution

———————

KEY (CORRECT ANSWERS)

1.	A		11.	B
2.	C		12.	A
3.	D		13.	D
4.	D		14.	D
5.	A		15.	B
6.	A		16.	B
7.	A		17.	B
8.	B		18.	D
9.	D		19.	A
10.	D		20.	B

21.	D
22.	D
23.	A
24.	D
25.	B

TEST 2

DIRECTIONS: Each question or incomplete statement is followed by several suggested answers or completions. Select the one that BEST answers the question or completes the statement. *PRINT THE LETTER OF THE CORRECT ANSWER IN THE SPACE AT THE RIGHT.*

Questions 1-7.

DIRECTIONS: Questions 1 through 7 are to be answered on the basis of the following paragraph.

FLAGGING RULES

When a track gang is going to work under flagging protection at a given location, the Desk Trainmaster of the division must be notified. Work on trainways must not be performed on operating tracks between 6:00 A.M. and 9:00 A.M., or between 4:00 P.M. and 7:00 P.M. A flagman must be selected from the list of flagmen qualified as such by the Assistant General Superintendent. No person acting as a flagman may be assigned any duties other than those of a flagman. For underground flagging signals, lighted lanterns must be used. Out of doors, flags at least 23" x 29" in dimensions must be used between sunrise and sunset. Moving a red light across the track is the prescribed stop signal under normal flagging conditions. Moving a white light up and down means proceed slowly. A red light must never be used to give a proceed signal. Moving a yellow light up and down is a signal to a motorman to proceed very slowly. On the track to be worked on, two yellow lights must be displayed at a point not less than 500 feet, nor more than 700 feet, in approach to the flagman's station. On any track where caution lights are displayed, one green light must be displayed a safe distance beyond the farthest point of work. Caution lights must be displayed on the right hand side of the track.

1. Before starting work on a track, the transit official who should be notified is the   1._____

    A. General Superintendent
    B. Assistant General Superintendent
    C. Desk Trainmaster
    D. Yardmaster

2. It is permissible to start work on an operating track at   2._____

    A. 8 A.M.   B. 11 A.M.   C. 8 P.M.   D. 6 P.M.

3. A flagman for a track gang MUST be selected from   3._____

    A. men on light duty   B. disabled men
    C. a list of qualified men   D. senior trackmen

4. The flagman who is protecting a working gang of trackmen   4._____

    A. should lend a hand when needed in heavy lifting
    B. should clean up the track area while awaiting trains
    C. must not be assigned to other duties
    D. can collect scrap iron while awaiting trains

5. The prescribed *stop* signal is given by moving a   5._____

    A. red light up and down   B. green light up and down
    C. red light across the tracks   D. green light across the tracks

6. The normal *proceed slowly* signal is given by moving a

    A. red light up and down
    B. white light up and down
    C. yellow light across the tracks
    D. green light across the tracks

6._

7. Of the following, an ACCEPTABLE distance between a work area and the yellow lights is _____ feet.

    A. 300   B. 600   C. 800   D. 1,000

7._

Questions 8-12.

DIRECTIONS: Questions 8 through 12 are to be answered on the basis of the following passage.

The handling of supplies is an important part of correctional administration. A good deal of planning and organization is involved in purchase, stock control, and issue of bulk supplies to the cell-block. This planning is meaningless, however, if the final link in the chain -- the cell-block officer who is in charge of distributing supplies to the inmates -- does not do his job in the proper way. First, when supplies are received, the officer himself should immediately check them or should personally supervise the checking, to make sure the count is correct. Nothing but trouble will result if an officer signs for 200 towels and discovers hours later that he is 20 towels short. Did the 20 towels *disappear,* or did they never arrive in the first place? Second, all supplies should be locked up until they are actually distributed. Third, the officer must keep accurate records when supplies are issued. Complaints will be kept to a minimum if the officer makes sure that each inmate has received the supplies to which he is entitled, and if the officer can tell from his records when it is time to reorder to prevent a shortage. Fourth, the officer should either issue the supplies himself or else personally supervise the issuing. It is unfair and unwise to put an inmate in charge of supplies without giving him adequate supervision. A small thing like a bar of soap does not mean much to most people, but it means a great deal to the inmate who cannot even shave or wash up unless he receives the soap that is supposed to be issued to him.

8. Which one of the following jobs is NOT mentioned by the above passage as the responsibility of a cellblock officer?

    A. Purchasing supplies
    B. Issuing supplies
    C. Counting supplies when they are delivered to the cell-block
    D. Keeping accurate records when supplies are issued

8._

9. The above passage says that supplies should be counted when they are delivered. Of the following, which is the BEST way of handling this job?

    A. The cellblock officer can wait until he has some free time, and then count them himself.
    B. An inmate can start counting them right away, even if the cellblock officer cannot supervise his work.
    C. The cellblock officer can personally supervise an inmate who counts the supplies when they are delivered.
    D. Two inmates can count them when they are delivered, supervising each other's work.

9._

10. The above passage gives an example concerning a delivery of 200 towels that turned out to be 20 towels short. The example is used to show that   10._____

    A. the missing towels were stolen
    B. the missing towels never arrived in the first place
    C. it is impossible to tell what happened to the missing towels because no count was made when they were delivered
    D. it does not matter that the missing towels were not accounted for because it is never possible to keep track of supplies accurately

11. The MAIN reason given by the above passage for making a record when supplies are issued is that keeping records   11._____

    A. will discourage inmates from stealing supplies
    B. is a way of making sure that each inmate receives the supplies to which he is entitled
    C. will show the officer's superiors that he is doing his job in the proper way
    D. will enable the inmates to help themselves to any supplies they need

12. The above passage says that it is unfair to put an inmate in charge of supplies without giving him adequate supervision.   12._____
Which of the following is the MOST likely explanation of why it would be *unfair* to do this?

    A. A privilege should not be given to one inmate unless it is given to all the other inmates too.
    B. It is wrong to make one inmate work when all the others can sit in their cells and do nothing.
    C. The cellblock officer should not be able to get out of doing a job by making an inmate do it for him.
    D. The inmate in charge of supplies could be put under pressure by other inmates to do them *special favors.*

Questions 13-17.

DIRECTIONS: Questions 13 through 17 are to be answered on the basis of the following passage.

    The typical correction official must make predictions about the probable future behavior of his charges in order to make judgments affecting those individuals. In learning to predict behavior, the results of scientific studies of inmate behavior can be of some use. Most studies that have been made show that older men tend to obey rules and regulations better than younger men, and tend to be more reliable in carrying out assigned jobs. Men who had good employment records on the outside also tend to be more reliable than men whose records show haphazard employment or unemployment. Oddly enough, men convicted of crimes of violence are less likely to be troublemakers than men convicted of burglary or other crimes involving stealth. While it might be expected that first offenders would be much less likely to be troublemakers than men with previous convictions, the difference between the two groups is not very great. It must be emphasized, however, that predictions based on a man's background are only likelihoods -- they are never certainties. A successful correction officer learns to give some weight to a man's background, but he should rely even more heavily on his own personal judgment of the individual in question. A good officer will develop in time a kind of sixth sense about human beings that is more reliable than any statistical predictions.

13. The above passage suggests that knowledge of scientific studies of inmate behavior would PROBABLY help the correction officer to   13.___

   A. make judgments that affect the inmates in his charge
   B. write reports on all major infractions of the rules
   C. accurately analyze how an inmate's behavior is determined by his background
   D. change the personalities of the individuals in his charge

14. According to the information in the above passage, which one of the following groups of inmates would tend to be MOST reliable in carrying out assigned jobs?   14.___

   A. Older men with haphazard employment records
   B. Older men with regular employment records
   C. Younger men with haphazard employment records
   D. Younger men with regular employment records

15. According to the information in the above passage, which of the following are MOST likely to be troublemakers?   15.___

   A. Older men convicted of crimes of violence
   B. Younger men convicted of crimes of violence
   C. Younger men convicted of crimes involving stealth
   D. First offenders convicted of crimes of violence

16. The above passage indicates that information about a man's background is   16.___

   A. a sure way of predicting his future behavior
   B. of no use at all in predicting his future behavior
   C. more useful in predicting behavior than a correction officer's expert judgment
   D. less reliable in predicting behavior than a correction officer's expert judgment

17. The above passage names two groups of inmates whose behavior might be expected to be quite different, but who in fact behave only slightly differently.
These two groups are   17.___

   A. older men and younger men
   B. first offenders and men with previous convictions
   C. men with good employment records and men with records of haphazard employment or unemployment
   D. men who obey the rules and men who do not

Questions 18-22.

DIRECTIONS: Questions 18 through 22 are to be answered on the basis of the following passage.

A large proportion of the people who are behind bars are not convicted criminals, but people who have been arrested and are being held until their trial in court. Experts have often pointed out that this detention system does not operate fairly. For instance, a person who can afford to pay bail usually will not get locked up. The theory of the bail system is that the person will make sure to show up in court when he is supposed to since he knows that otherwise he will forfeit his bail -- he will lose the money he put up. Sometimes a person who can show that he is a stable citizen with a job and a family will be released on *personal recognizance* (without bail). The result is that the well-to-do, the employed, and the family men can often avoid the detention system. The people who do wind up in detention tend to be the poor, the unemployed, the single, and the young.

18. According to the above passage, people who are put behind bars   18.____

    A.   are almost always dangerous criminals
    B.   include many innocent people who have been arrested by mistake
    C.   are often people who have been arrested but have not yet come to trial
    D.   are all poor people who tend to be young and single

19. The above passage says that the detention system works UNFAIRLY against people   19.____

    A.   rich   B.   married   C.   old   D.   unemployed

20. The above passage uses the expression *forfeit his bail.* Even if you have not seen the   20.____
word *forfeit* before, you could figure out from the way it is used in the passage that *forfeiting* PROBABLY means _____ something.

    A.   losing track of   B.   giving up
    C.   finding   D.   avoiding

21. When someone is released on *personal recognizance,* this means that   21.____

    A.   the judge knows that he is innocent
    B.   he does not have to show up for a trial
    C.   he has a record of previous convictions
    D.   he does not have to pay bail

22. Suppose that two men were booked on the same charge at the same time, and that the   22.____
same bail was set for both of them. One man was able to put up bail, and he was released. The second man was not able to put up bail, and he was held in detention. The reader of the above passage would MOST likely feel that this result is

    A.   *unfair,* because it does not have any relation to guilt or innocence
    B.   *unfair,* because the first man deserves severe punishment
    C.   *fair,* because the first man is obviously innocent
    D.   *fair,* because the law should be tougher on poor people than on rich people

Questions 23-25.

DIRECTIONS: Questions 23 through 25 are to be answered on the basis of the information contained in the following paragraph,

Group counseling may contain potentialities of an extraordinary character for the philosophy and especially the management and operation of the adult correctional institution. Primarily, the change may be based upon the valued and respected participation of the rank-and-file of employees in the treatment program. Group counseling provides new treatment functions for correctional workers. The older, more conventional duties and activities of correctional officers, teachers, maintenance foremen, and other employees, which they currently perform, may be fortified and improved by their participation in group counseling. Psychologists, psychiatrists, and classification officers may also need to revise their attitudes toward others on the staff and toward their own procedure in treating inmates to accord with the new type of treatment program which may evolve if group counseling were to become accepted practice in the prison. The primary locale of the psychological treatment program may move from the clinical center to all places in the institution where inmates are in contact with employees. The thoughtful guidance and steering of the program, figuratively its pilot-house, may still be the clinical center. The actual points of contact of the treatment program will, however, be wherever inmates are in personal relationship, no matter how superficial, with employees of the prison.

23. According to the above paragraph, a basic change that may be brought about by the introduction of a group counseling program into an adult correctional institution would be that the   23.____

    A. educational standards for correctional employees would be raised
    B. management of the institution would have to be selected primarily on the basis of ability to understand and apply the counseling program
    C. older and conventional duties of correctional employees would assume less importance
    D. rank-and-file employees would play an important part in the treatment program for inmates

24. According to the above paragraph, the one of the following that is NOT mentioned specifically as a change that may be required by or result from the introduction of group counseling in an adult correctional institution is a change in the   24.____

    A. attitude of the institution's classification officers toward their own procedures in treating inmates
    B. attitudes of the institution's psychologists toward correction officers
    C. place where the treatment program is planned and from which it is directed
    D. principal place where the psychological treatment program makes actual contact with the inmate

25. According to the above paragraph, under a program of group counseling in an adult correctional institution, treatment of inmates takes place   25.___

    A. as soon as they are admitted to the prison
    B. chiefly in the clinical center
    C. mainly where inmates are in continuing close and personal relationship with the technical staff
    D. wherever inmates come in contact with prison employees

---

KEY (CORRECT ANSWERS)

1.	C		11.	B
2.	B		12.	D
3.	C		13.	A
4.	C		14.	B
5.	C		15.	C
6.	B		16.	D
7.	B		17.	B
8.	A		18.	C
9.	C		19.	D
10.	C		20.	B

21. D
22. A
23. D
24. C
25. D

———

PREPARING WRITTEN MATERIAL

PARAGRAPH REARRANGEMENT
COMMENTARY

The sentences which follow are in scrambled order. You are to rearrange them in proper order and indicate the letter choice containing the correct answer at the space at the right.

Each group of sentences in this section is actually a paragraph presented in scrambled order. Each sentence in the group has a place in that paragraph; no sentence is to be left out. You are to read each group of sentences and decide upon the best order in which to put the sentences so as to form as well-organized paragraph.

The questions in this section measure the ability to solve a problem when all the facts relevant to its solution are not given.

More specifically, certain positions of responsibility and authority require the employee to discover connections between events sometimes, apparently, unrelated. In order to do this, the employee will find it necessary to correctly infer that unspecified events have probably occurred or are likely to occur. This ability becomes especially important when action must be taken on incomplete information.

Accordingly, these questions require competitors to choose among several suggested alternatives, each of which presents a different sequential arrangement of the events. Competitors must choose the MOST logical of the suggested sequences.

In order to do so, they may be required to draw on general knowledge to infer missing concepts or events that are essential to sequencing the given events. Competitors should be careful to infer only what is essential to the sequence. The plausibility of the wrong alternatives will always require the inclusion of unlikely events or of additional chains of events which are NOT essential to sequencing the given events.

It's very important to remember that you are looking for the best of the four possible choices, and that the best choice of all may not even be one of the answers you're given to choose from.

There is no one right way to solve these problems. Many people have found it helpful to first write out the order of the sentences, as they would have arranged them, on their scrap paper before looking at the possible answers. If their optimum answer is there, this can save them some time. If it isn't, this method can still give insight into solving the problem. Others find it most helpful to just go through each of the possible choices, contrasting each as they go along. You should use whatever method feels comfortable, and works, for you.

While most of these types of questions are not that difficult, we've added a higher percentage of the difficult type, just to give you more practice. Usually there are only one or two questions on this section that contain such subtle distinctions that you're unable to answer confidently, and you then may find yourself stuck deciding between two possible choices, neither of which you're sure about.

EXAMINATION SECTION
TEST 1

DIRECTIONS: Each question consists of several sentences which can be arranged in a logical sequence. For each question, select the choice which places the numbered sentences in the MOST logical sequence. *PRINT THE LETTER OF THE CORRECT ANSWER IN THE SPACE AT THE RIGHT.*

1.   I.   A body was found in the woods.
    II.   A man proclaimed innocence.
    III. The owner of a gun was located.
    IV.   A gun was traced.
    V.   The owner of a gun was questioned.
    The CORRECT answer is:

    A. IV, III, V, II, I   B. II, I, IV, III, V
    C. I, IV, III, V, II   D. I, III, V, II, IV
    E. I, II, IV, III, V

1.____

2.   I.   A man was in a hunting accident.
    II.   A man fell down a flight of steps.
    III. A man lost his vision in one eye.
    IV.   A man broke his leg.
    V.   A man had to walk with a cane.
    The CORRECT answer is:

    A. II, IV, V, I, III   B. IV, V, I, III, II
    C. III, I, IV, V, II   D. I, III, V, II, IV
    E. I, III, II, IV, V

2.____

3.   I.   A man is offered a new job.
    II.   A woman is offered a new job.
    III. A man works as a waiter.
    IV.   A woman works as a waitress.
    V.   A woman gives notice.
    The CORRECT answer is:

    A. IV, II, V, III, I   B. IV, II, V, I, III
    C. II, IV, V, III, I   D. III, I, IV, II, V
    E. IV, III, II, V, I

3.____

4.   I.   A train left the station late.
    II.   A man was late for work.
    III. A man lost his job.
    IV.   Many people complained because the train was late.
    V.   There was a traffic jam.
    The CORRECT answer is:

    A. V, II, I, IV, III   B. V, I, IV, II, III
    C. V, I, II, IV, III   D. I, V, IV, II, III
    E. II, I, IV, V, III

4.____

5.   I.   The burden of proof as to each issue is determined before trial and remains upon   5.____
the same party throughout the trial.

    II.   The jury is at liberty to believe one witness' testimony as against a number of
contradictory witnesses.

    III. In a civil case, the party bearing the burden of proof is required to prove his con-
tention by a fair preponderance of the evidence.

    IV. However, it must be noted that a fair preponderance of evidence does not neces-
sarily mean a greater number of witnesses.

    V.   The burden of proof is the burden which rests upon one of the parties to an
action to persuade the trier of the facts, generally the jury, that a proposition he
asserts is true.

    VI. If the evidence is equally balanced, or if it leaves the jury in such doubt as to be
unable to decide the controversy either way, judgment must be given against the
party upon whom the burden of proof rests.

The CORRECT answer is:

A. III, II, V, IV, I, VI   B. I, II,VI,V,III,IV
C. III, IV, V, I, II, VI   D. V, I, III,VI, IV, II
E. I,V, III, VI, IV, II

6.   I.   If a parent is without assets and is unemployed, he cannot be convicted of the   6.____
crime of non-support of a child.

    II.   The term *sufficient ability* has been held to mean sufficient financial ability.

    III. It does not matter if his unemployment is by choice or unavoidable circum-
stances.

    IV. If he fails to take any steps at all, he may be liable to prosecution for endangering
the welfare of a child.

    V.   Under the penal law, a parent is responsible for the support of his minor child
only if the parent is of *sufficient ability*.

    VI. An indigent parent may meet his obligation by borrowing money or by seeking
aid under the provisions of the Social Welfare Law.

The CORRECT answer is:

A. VI, I, V, III, II, IV   B. I, III, V, II, IV, VI
C. V, II, I, III, VI, IV   D. I, VI, IV, V, II, III
E. II, V, I, III, VI, IV

7.   I.   Consider, for example, the case of a rabble rouser who urges a group of twenty   7.____
people to go out and break the windows of a nearby factory.

    II.   Therefore, the law fills the indicated gap with the crime of *inciting to riot*.

    III. A person is considered guilty of inciting to riot when he urges ten or more per-
sons to engage in tumultuous and violent conduct of a kind likely to create public
alarm.

    IV. However, if he has not obtained the cooperation of at least four people, he can-
not be charged with unlawful assembly.

    V.   The charge of inciting to riot was added to the law to cover types of conduct
which cannot be classified as either the crime of *riot* or the crime of *unlawful
assembly*.

    VI. If he acquires the acquiescence of at least four of them, he is guilty of unlawful
assembly even if the project does not materialize.

The CORRECT answer is:

A. III, V, I, VI, IV, II B. V, I, IV, VI, II, III
C. III, IV, I, V, II, VI D. V, I, IV, VI, III, II
E. V, III, I, VI, IV, II

8. I. If, however, the rebuttal evidence presents an issue of credibility, it is for the jury to determine whether the presumption has, in fact, been destroyed. 8.____
   II. Once sufficient evidence to the contrary is introduced, the presumption disappears from the trial.
   III. The effect of a presumption is to place the burden upon the adversary to come forward with evidence to rebut the presumption.
   IV. When a presumption is overcome and ceases to exist in the case, the fact or facts which gave rise to the presumption still remain.
   V. Whether a presumption has been overcome is ordinarily a question for the court.
   VI. Such information may furnish a basis for a logical inference.
   The CORRECT answer is:

   A. IV, VI, II, V, I, III B. III, II, V, I, IV, VI
   C. V, III, VI, IV, II, I D. V, IV, I, II, VI, III
   E. II, III, V, I, IV, VI

9. I. An executive may answer a letter by writing his reply on the face of the letter itself instead of having a return letter typed. 9.____
   II. This procedure is efficient because it saves the executive's time, the typist's time, and saves office file space.
   III. Copying machines are used in small offices as well as large offices to save time and money in making brief replies to business letters.
   IV. A copy is made on a copying machine to go into the company files, while the original is mailed back to the sender.
   The CORRECT answer is:

   A. I, II, IV, III B. I, IV, II, III
   C. III, I, IV, II D. III, IV, II, I

10. I. Most organizations favor one of the types but always include the others to a lesser degree. 10.____
    II. However, we can detect a definite trend toward greater use of symbolic control.
    III. We suggest that our local police agencies are today primarily utilizing material control.
    IV. Control can be classified into three types: physical, material, and symbolic.
    The CORRECT answer is:

    A. IV, II, III, I B. II, I, IV, III
    C. III, IV, II, I D. IV, I, III, II

11. I. Project residents had first claim to this use, followed by surrounding neighborhood children. 11.____
    II. By contrast, recreation space within the project's interior was found to be used more often by both groups.
    III. Studies of the use of project grounds in many cities showed grounds left open for public use were neglected and unused, both by residents and by members of the surrounding community.

IV. Project residents had clearly laid claim to the play spaces, setting up and enforc-ing unwritten rules for use.

V. Each group, by experience, found their activities easily disrupted by other groups, and their claim to the use of space for recreation difficult to enforce.

The CORRECT answer is:

A. IV, V, I, II, III   B. V, II, IV, III, I
C. I, IV, III, II, V   D. III, V, II, IV, I

12.   I. They do not consider the problems correctable within the existing subsidy formula and social policy of accepting all eligible applicants regardless of social behavior and lifestyle.   12.___

II. A recent survey, however, indicated that tenants believe these problems correct-able by local housing authorities and management within the existing financial formula.

III. Many of the problems and complaints concerning public housing management and design have created resentment between the tenant and the landlord.

IV. This same survey indicated that administrators and managers do not agree with the tenants.

The CORRECT answer is:

A. II, I, III, IV   B. I, III, IV, II
C. III, II, IV, I   D. IV, II, I, III

13.   I. In single-family residences, there is usually enough distance between tenants to prevent occupants from annoying one another.   13.___

II. For example, a certain small percentage of tenant families has one or more members addicted to alcohol.

III. While managers believe in the right of individuals to live as they choose, the manager becomes concerned when the pattern of living jeopardizes others' rights.

IV. Still others turn night into day, staging lusty entertainments which carry on into the hours when most tenants are trying to sleep.

V. In apartment buildings, however, tenants live so closely together that any misbe-havior can result in unpleasant living conditions.

VI. Other families engage in violent argument.

The CORRECT answer is:

A. III, II, V, IV, VI, I   B. I, V, II, VI, IV, III
C. II, V, IV, I, III, VI   D. IV, II, V, VI, III, I

14.   I. Congress made the commitment explicit in the Housing Act of 1949, establishing as a national goal the realization of *a decent home and suitable environment for every American family.*   14.___

II. The result has been that the goal of decent home and suitable environment is still as far distant as ever for the disadvantaged urban family.

III. In spite of this action by Congress, federal housing programs have continued to be fragmented and grossly underfunded.

IV. The passage of the National Housing Act signalled a new federal commitment to provide housing for the nation's citizens.

The CORRECT answer is:

A. I, IV, III, II   B. IV, I, III, II
C. IV, I, II, III   D. II, IV, I, III

15.
   I.   The greater expense does not necessarily involve *exploitation,* but it is often perceived as exploitative and unfair by those who are aware of the price differences involved, but unaware of operating costs.

   II.   Ghetto residents believe they are *exploited* by local merchants, and evidence substantiates some of these beliefs.

   III.   However, stores in low-income areas were more likely to be small independents, which could not achieve the economies available to supermarket chains and were, therefore, more likely to charge higher prices, and the customers were more likely to buy smaller-sized packages which are more expensive per unit of measure.

   IV.   A study conducted in one city showed that distinctly higher prices were charged for goods sold in ghetto stores than in other areas.

The CORRECT answer is:

A. IV, II, I, III
C. II, IV, III, I

B. IV, I, III, II
D. II, III, IV, I

15.____

KEY (CORRECT ANSWERS)

1.	C	6.	C
2.	E	7.	A
3.	B	8.	B
4.	B	9.	C
5.	D	10.	D

11.	D
12.	C
13.	B
14.	B
15.	C

PREPARING WRITTEN MATERIALS

EXAMINATION SECTION

TEST 1

DIRECTIONS: Each question consists of a sentence which may be classified appropriately under one of the following four categories:
  A. Incorrect because of faulty grammar or sentence structure.
  B. Incorrect because of faulty punctuation.
  C. Incorrect because of faulty spelling or capitalization.
  D. Correct

Examine each sentence carefully. Then, in the space at the right, print the capital letter preceding the option which is the BEST of the four suggested above. All incorrect sentences contain only one type of error. Consider a sentence correct if it contains none of the types of errors mentioned, although there may be other correct ways of expressing the same thought.

1. The fire apparently started in the storeroom, which is usually locked.   1.____

2. On approaching the victim two bruises were noticed by this officer.   2.____

3. The officer, who was there examined the report with great care.   3.____

4. Each employee in the office had a separate desk.   4.____

5. The suggested procedure is similar to the one now in use.   5.____

6. No one was more pleased with the new procedure than the chauffeur.   6.____

7. He tried to pursuade her to change the procedure.   7.____

8. The total of the expenses charged to petty cash were high.   8.____

9. An understanding between him and I was finally reached.   9.____

10. It was at the supervisor's request that the clerk agreed to postpone his vacation.   10.____

11. We do not believe that it is necessary for both he and the clerk to attend the conference.   11.____

12. All employees, who display perseverance, will be given adequate recognition.   12.____

13. He regrets that some of us employees are dissatisfied with our new assignments.   13.____

14. "Do you think that the raise was merited," asked the supervisor?   14.____

15. The new manual of procedure is a valuable supplament to our rules and   15.____
    regulation.

16. The typist admitted that she had attempted to pursuade the other employees   16.____
    to assist her in her work.

17. The supervisor asked that all amendments to the regulations be handled by   17.____
    you and I.

18. They told both he and I that the prisoner had escaped.   18.____

19. Any superior officer, who, disregards the just complaints of his subordinates,   19.____
    is remiss in the performance of his duty.

20. Only those members of the national organization who resided in the Middle   20.____
    west attended the conference in Chicago.

21. We told him to give the investigation assignment to whoever was available.   21.____

22. Please do not disappoint and embarass us by not appearing in court.   22.____

23. Despite the efforts of the Supervising mechanic, the elevator could not be   23.____
    started.

24. The U.S. Weather Bureau, weather record for the accident date was checked.   24.____

———————

KEY (CORRECT ANSWERS)

1.	D		11.	A
2.	A		12.	B
3.	B		13.	D
4.	D		14.	B
5.	D		15.	C
6.	D		16.	C
7.	C		17.	A
8.	A		18.	A
9.	A		19.	B
10.	D		20.	C

21.	D
22.	C
23.	C
24.	B

TEST 2

DIRECTIONS: Each question consists of a sentence. Some of the sentences contain errors in English grammar or usage, punctuation, spelling, or capitalization. A sentence does not contain an error simply because it could be written in a different manner. Choose answer:
- A. If the sentence contains an error in English grammar or usage.
- B. if the sentence contains an error in punctuation.
- C. If the sentence contains an error in spelling or capitalization
- D. If the sentence does not contain any errors.

1. The severity of the sentence prescribed by contemporary statutes—including both the former and the revised New York Penal Laws—do not depend on what crime was intended by the offender.   1._____

2. It is generally recognized that two defects in the early law of attempt played a part in the birth of burglary: (1) immunity from prosecution for conduct short of the last act before completion of the crime, and (2) the relatively minor penalty imposed for an attempt (it being a common law misdemeanor) vis-à-vis the completed offense.   2._____

3. The first sentence of the statute is applicable to employees who enter their place of employment, invited guests, and all other persons who have an express or implied license or privilege to enter the premises.   3._____

4. Contemporary criminal codes in the United States generally divide burglary into various degrees, differentiating the categories according to place, time and other attendent circumstances.   4._____

5. The assignment was completed in record time but the payroll for it has not yet been prepaid.   5._____

6. The operator, on the other hand, is willing to learn me how to use the mimeograph.   6._____

7. She is the prettiest of the three sisters.   7._____

8. She doesn't know; if the mail has arrived.   8._____

9. The doorknob of the office door is broke.   9._____

10. Although the department's supply of scratch pads and stationery have diminished considerably, the allotment for our division has not been reduced.   10._____

11. You have not told us whom you wish to designate as your secretary.   11._____

12. Upon reading the minutes of the last meeting, the new proposal was taken up for consideration.   12._____

13. Before beginning the discussion, we locked the door as a precautionery measure.   13._____

14. The supervisor remarked, "Only those clerks, who perform routine work, are permitted to take a rest period."   14._____

15. Not only will this duplicating machine make accurate copies, but it will also produce a quantity of work equal to fifteen transcribing typists.   15._____

16. "Mr. Jones," said the supervisor, "we regret our inability to grant you an extention of your leave of absence."   16._____

17. Although the employees find the work monotonous and fatigueing, they rarely complain.   17._____

18. We completed the tabulation of the receipts on time despite the fact that Miss Smith our fastest operator was absent for over a week.   18._____

19. The reaction of the employees who attended the meeting, as well as the reaction of those who did not attend, indicates clearly that the schedule is satisfactory to everyone concerned.   19._____

20. Of the two employees, the one in our office is the most efficient.   20._____

21. No one can apply or even understand, the new rules and regulations.   21._____

22. A large amount of supplies were stored in the empty office.   22._____

23. If an employee is occassionally asked to work overtime, he should do so willingly.   23._____

24. It is true that the new procedures are difficult to use but, we are certain that you will learn them quickly.   24._____

25. The office manager said that he did not know who would be given a large allotment under the new plan.   25._____

———————

KEY (CORRECT ANSWERS)

1.	A		11.	D
2.	D		12.	A
3.	D		13.	C
4.	C		14.	B
5.	C		15.	A
6.	A		16.	C
7.	D		17.	C
8.	B		18.	B
9.	A		19.	D
10.	A		20.	A

21.	B
22.	A
23.	C
24.	B
25.	D

TEST 3

DIRECTIONS: Each of the following sentences may be classified MOST appropriately under one of the following categories:
  A. Faulty because of incorrect grammar
  B. Faulty because of incorrect punctuation
  C. Faulty because of incorrect capitalization
  D. Correct

Examine each sentence carefully. Then, in the space at the right, print the capital letter preceding the option which is the BEST of the four suggested above. All incorrect sentence contain but one type of error. Consider a sentence correct if it contains none of the types of errors mentioned, even though there may be other correct ways of expressing the same thought.

1. The desk, as well as the chairs, were moved out of the office.   1._____

2. The clerk whose production was greatest for the month won a day's vacation as first prize.   2._____

3. Upon entering the room, the employees were found hard at work at their desks.   3._____

4. John Smith our new employee always arrives at work on time.   4._____

5. Punish whoever is guilty of stealing the money.   5._____

6. Intelligent and persistent effort lead to success no matter what the job may be.   6._____

7. The secretary asked, "can you call again at three o'clock?"   7._____

8. He told us, that if the report was not accepted at the next meeting, it would have to be rewritten.   8._____

9. He would not have sent the letter if he had known that it would cause so much excitement.   9._____

10. We all looked forward to him coming to visit us.   10._____

11. If you find that you are unable to complete the assignment please notify me as soon as possible.   11._____

12. Every girl in the office went home on time but me; there was still some work for me to finish.   12._____

13. He wanted to know who the letter was addressed to, Mr. Brown or Mr. Smith.   13._____

14. "Mr. Jones, he said, please answer this letter as soon as possible."   14._____

15. The new clerk had an unusual accent inasmuch as he was born and educated in the south.   15.____

16. Although he is younger than her, he earns a higher salary.   16.____

17. Neither of the two administrators are going to attend the conference being held in Washington, D.C.   17.____

18. Since Miss Smith and Miss Jones have more experience than us, they have been given more responsible duties.   18.____

19. Mr. Shaw the supervisor of the stock room maintains an inventory of stationery and office supplies.   19.____

20. Inasmuch as this matter affects both you and I, we should take joint action.   20.____

21. Who do you think will be able to perform this highly technical work?   21.____

22. Of the two employees, John is considered the most competent.   22.____

23. He is not coming home on tuesday; we expect him next week.   23.____

24. Stenographers, as well as typists must be able to type rapidly and accurately.   24.____

25. Having been placed in the safe we were sure that the money would not be stolen.   25.____

————

KEY (CORRECT ANSWERS)

1.	A		11.	B
2.	D		12.	D
3.	A		13.	A
4.	B		14.	B
5.	D		15.	C
6.	A		16.	A
7.	C		17.	A
8.	B		18.	A
9.	D		19.	B
10.	A		20.	A

21.	D
22.	A
23.	C
24.	B
25.	A

TEST 4

DIRECTIONS: Each of the following sentences consist of four sentences lettered A, B, C, and D. One of the sentences in each group contains an error in grammar or punctuation. Indicate the INCORRECT sentence in each group. *PRINT THE LETTER OF THE CORRECT ANSWER IN THE SPACE AT THE RIGHT.*

1. A. Give the message to whoever is on duty.
    B. The teacher who's pupil won first prize presented the award.
    C. Between you and me, I don't expect the program to succeed.
    D. His running to catch the bus caused the accident.

    1.____

2. A. The process, which was patented only last year is already obsolete.
    B. His interest in science (which continues to the present) led him to convert his basement into a laboratory.
    C. He described the book as "verbose, repetitious, and bombastic".
    D. Our new director will need to possess three qualities: vision, patience, and fortitude.

    2.____

3. A. The length of ladder trucks varies considerably.
    B. The probationary fireman reported to the officer to who he was assigned.
    C. The lecturer emphasized the need for we firemen to be punctual.
    D. Neither the officers nor the members of the company knew about the new procedure.

    3.____

4. A. Ham and eggs is the specialty of the house.
    B. He is one of the students who are on probation.
    C. Do you think that either one of us have a chance to be nominated for president of the class?
    D. I assume that either he was to be in charge or you were.

    4.____

5. A. Its a long road that has no turn.
    B. To run is more tiring than to walk.
    C. We have been assigned three new reports: namely, the statistical summary, the narrative summary, and the budgetary summary.
    D. Had the first payment been made in January, the second would be due in April.

    5.____

6. A. Each employer has his own responsibilities.
    B. If a person speaks correctly, they make a good impression.
    C. Every one of the operators has had her vacation.
    D. Has anybody filed his report?

    6.____

7. A. The manager, with all his salesmen, was obliged to go.
    B. Who besides them is to sign the agreement?
    C. One report without the others is incomplete.
    D. Several clerks, as well as the proprietor, was injured.

    7.____

8. A. A suspension of these activities is expected.   8.____
    B. The machine is economical because first cost and upkeep are low.
    C. A knowledge of stenography and filing are required for this position.
    D. The condition in which the goods were received shows that the packing
        was not done properly.

9. A. There seems to be a great many reasons for disagreement.   9.____
    B. It does not seem possible that they could have failed.
    C. Have there always been too few applicants for these positions?
    D. There is no excuse for these errors.

10. A. We shall be pleased to answer your question.   10.____
    B. Shall we plan the meeting for Saturday?
    C. I will call you promptly at seven.
    D. Can I borrow your book after you have read it?

11. A. You are as capable as I.   11.____
    B. Everyone is willing to sign but him and me.
    C. As for he and his assistant, I cannot praise them too highly.
    D. Between you and me, I think he will be dismissed.

12. A. Our competitors bid above us last week.   12.____
    B. The survey which was began last year has not yet been completed.
    C. The operators had shown that they understood their instructions.
    D. We have never ridden over worse roads.

13. A. Who did they say was responsible?   13.____
    B. Whom did you suspect?
    C. Who do you suppose it was?
    D. Whom do you mean?

14. A. Of the two propositions, this is the worse.   14.____
    B. Which report do you consider the best—the one in January or the one in
        July?
    C. I believe this is the most practicable of the many plans submitted.
    D. He is the youngest employee in the organization.

15. A. The firm had but three orders last week.   15.____
    B. That doesn't really seem possible.
    C. After twenty years scarcely none of the old business remains.
    D. Has he done nothing about it?

KEY (CORRECT ANSWERS)

1.	B	6.	B	11.	C
2.	A	7.	D	12.	B
3.	C	8.	C	13.	A
4.	C	9.	A	14.	B
5.	A	10.	D	15.	C

———

PREPARING WRITTEN MATERIAL

EXAMINATION SECTION
TEST 1

DIRECTIONS: Each question or incomplete statement is followed by several suggested answers or completions. Select the one that BEST answers the question or completes the statement. *PRINT THE LETTER OF THE CORRECT ANSWER IN THE SPACE AT THE RIGHT.*

1. The one of the following sentences which is LEAST acceptable from the viewpoint of correct usage is:

    1._____

    A. The police thought the fugitive to be him.
    B. The criminals set a trap for whoever would fall into it.
    C. It is ten years ago since the fugitive fled from the city.
    D. The lecturer argued that criminals are usually cowards.
    E. The police removed four bucketfuls of earth from the scene of the crime.

2. The one of the following sentences which is LEAST acceptable from the viewpoint of correct usage is:

    2._____

    A. The patrolman scrutinized the report with great care.
    B. Approaching the victim of the assault, two bruises were noticed by the patrolman.
    C. As soon as I had broken down the door, I stepped into the room.
    D. I observed the accused loitering near the building, which was closed at the time.
    E. The storekeeper complained that his neighbor was guilty of violating a local ordinance.

3. The one of the following sentences which is LEAST acceptable from the viewpoint of correct usage is:

    3._____

    A. I realized immediately that he intended to assault the woman, so I disarmed him.
    B. It was apparent that Mr. Smith's explanation contained many inconsistencies.
    C. Despite the slippery condition of the street, he managed to stop the vehicle before injuring the child.
    D. Not a single one of them wish, despite the damage to property, to make a formal complaint.
    E. The body was found lying on the floor.

4. The one of the following sentences which contains NO error in usage is:

    4._____

    A. After the robbers left, the proprietor stood tied in his chair for about two hours before help arrived.
    B. In the cellar I found the watchmans' hat and coat.
    C. The persons living in adjacent apartments stated that they had heard no unusual noises.
    D. Neither a knife or any firearms were found in the room.
    E. Walking down the street, the shouting of the crowd indicated that something was wrong.

5. The one of the following sentences which contains NO error in usage is: 5.____

    A. The policeman lay a firm hand on the suspect's shoulder.
    B. It is true that neither strength nor agility are the most important requirement for a good patrolman.
    C. Good citizens constantly strive to do more than merely comply the restraints imposed by society.
    D. No decision was made as to whom the prize should be awarded.
    E. Twenty years is considered a severe sentence for a felony.

6. Which of the following is NOT expressed in standard English usage? 6.____

    A. The victim reached a pay-phone booth and manages to call police headquarters.
    B. By the time the call was received, the assailant had left the scene.
    C. The victim has been a respected member of the community for the past eleven years.
    D. Although the lighting was bad and the shadows were deep, the storekeeper caught sight of the attacker.
    E. Additional street lights have since been installed, and the patrols have been strengthened.

7. Which of the following is NOT expressed in standard English usage? 7.____

    A. The judge upheld the attorney's right to question the witness about the missing glove.
    B. To be absolutely fair to all parties is the jury's chief responsibility.
    C. Having finished the report, a loud noise in the next room startled the sergeant.
    D. The witness obviously enjoyed having played a part in the proceedings.
    E. The sergeant planned to assign the case to whoever arrived first.

8. In which of the following is a word misused? 8.____

    A. As a matter of principle, the captain insisted that the suspect's partner be brought for questioning.
    B. The principle suspect had been detained at the station house for most of the day.
    C. The principal in the crime had no previous criminal record, but his closest associate had been convicted of felonies on two occasions.
    D. The interest payments had been made promptly, but the firm had been drawing upon the principal for these payments.
    E. The accused insisted that his high school principal would furnish him a character reference.

9. Which of the following statements is ambiguous? 9.____

    A. Mr. Sullivan explained why Mr. Johnson had been dismissed from his job.
    B. The storekeeper told the patrolman he had made a mistake.
    C. After waiting three hours, the patients in the doctor's office were sent home.
    D. The janitor's duties were to maintain the building in good shape and to answer tenants' complaints.
    E. The speed limit should, in my opinion, be raised to sixty miles an hour on that stretch of road.

10. In which of the following is the punctuation or capitalization faulty?   10.____

    A. The accident occurred at an intersection in the Kew Gardens section of Queens, near the bus stop.

    B. The sedan, not the convertible, was struck in the side.

    C. Before any of the patrolmen had left the police car received an important message from headquarters.

    D. The dog that had been stolen was returned to his master, John Dempsey, who lived in East Village.

    E. The letter had been sent to 12 Hillside Terrace, Rutland, Vermont 05701.

Questions 11-25.

DIRECTIONS: Questions 11 through 25 are to be answered in accordance with correct English usage; that is, standard English rather than nonstandard or substandard. Nonstandard and substandard English includes words or expressions usually classified as slang, dialect, illiterate, etc., which are not generally accepted as correct in current written communication. Standard English also requires clarity, proper punctuation and capitalization and appropriate use of words. Write the letter of the sentence NOT expressed in standard English usage in the space at the right.

11. A. There were three witnesses to the accident.   11.____
    B. At least three witnesses were found to testify for the plaintiff.
    C. Three of the witnesses who took the stand was uncertain about the defendant's competence to drive.
    D. Only three witnesses came forward to testify for the plaintiff.
    E. The three witnesses to the accident were pedestrians.

12. A. The driver had obviously drunk too many martinis before leaving for home.   12.____
    B. The boy who drowned had swum in these same waters many times before.
    C. The petty thief had stolen a bicycle from a private driveway before he was apprehended.
    D. The detectives had brung in the heroin shipment they intercepted.
    E. The passengers had never ridden in a converted bus before.

13. A. Between you and me, the new platoon plan sounds like a good idea.   13.____
    B. Money from an aunt's estate was left to his wife and he.
    C. He and I were assigned to the same patrol for the first time in two months.
    D. Either you or he should check the front door of that store.
    E. The captain himself was not sure of the witness's reliability.

14. A. The alarm had scarcely begun to ring when the explosion occurred.   14.____
    B. Before the firemen arrived on the scene, the second story had been destroyed.
    C. Because of the dense smoke and heat, the firemen could hardly approach the now-blazing structure.
    D. According to the patrolman's report, there wasn't nobody in the store when the explosion occurred.
    E. The sergeant's suggestion was not at all unsound, but no one agreed with him.

15.   A.   The driver and the passenger they were both found to be intoxicated.   15.____
       B.   The driver and the passenger talked slowly and not too clearly.
       C.   Neither the driver nor his passengers were able to give a coherent account of the
            accident.
       D.   In a corner of the room sat the passenger, quietly dozing.
       E.   The driver finally told a strange and unbelievable story, which the passenger con-
            tradicted.

16.   A.   Under the circumstances I decided not to continue my examination of the pre-   16.____
            mises.
       B.   There are many difficulties now not comparable with those existing in 1960.
       C.   Friends of the accused were heard to announce that the witness had better been
            away on the day of the trial.
       D.   The two criminals escaped in the confusion that followed the explosion.
       E.   The aged man was struck by the considerateness of the patrolman's offer.

17.   A.   An assemblage of miscellaneous weapons lay on the table.   17.____
       B.   Ample opportunities were given to the defendant to obtain counsel.
       C.   The speaker often alluded to his past experience with youthful offenders in the
            armed forces.
       D.   The sudden appearance of the truck aroused my suspicions.
       E.   Her studying had a good affect on her grades in high school.

18.   A.   He sat down in the theater and began to watch the movie.   18.____
       B.   The girl had ridden horses since she was four years old.
       C.   Application was made on behalf of the prosecutor to cite the witness for con-
            tempt.
       D.   The bank robber, with his two accomplices, were caught in the act.
       E.   His story is simply not credible.

19.   A.   The angry boy said that he did not like those kind of friends.   19.____
       B.   The merchant's financial condition was so precarious that he felt he must avail
            himself of any offer of assistance.
       C.   He is apt to promise more than he can perform.
       D.   Looking at the messy kitchen, the housewife felt like crying.
       E.   A clerk was left in charge of the stolen property.

20.   A.   His wounds were aggravated by prolonged exposure to sub-freezing temperatures.   20.____
       B.   The prosecutor remarked that the witness was not averse to changing his story
            each time he was interviewed.
       C.   The crime pattern indicated that the burglars were adapt in the handling of explo-
            sives.
       D.   His rigid adherence to a fixed plan brought him into renewed conflict with his
            subordinates.
       E.   He had anticipated that the sentence would be delivered by noon.

21.   A. The whole arraignment procedure is badly in need of revision.   21._____
      B. After his glasses were broken in the fight, he would of gone to the optometrist if he could.
      C. Neither Tom nor Jack brought his lunch to work.
      D. He stood aside until the quarrel was over.
      E. A statement in the psychiatrist's report disclosed that the probationer vowed to have his revenge.

22.   A. His fiery and intemperate speech to the striking employees fatally affected any   22._____
chance of a future reconciliation.
      B. The wording of the statute has been variously construed.
      C. The defendant's attorney, speaking in the courtroom, called the official a dema-gogue who contempuously disregarded the judge's orders.
      D. The baseball game is likely to be the most exciting one this year.
      E. The mother divided the cookies among her two children.

23.   A. There was only a bed and a dresser in the dingy room.   23._____
      B. John is one of the few students that have protested the new rule.
      C. It cannot be argued that the child's testimony is negligible; it is, on the contrary, of the greatest importance.
      D. The basic criterion for clearance was so general that officials resolved any doubts in favor of dismissal.
      E. Having just returned from a long vacation, the officer found the city unbearably hot.

24.   A. The librarian ought to give more help to small children.   24._____
      B. The small boy was criticized by the teacher because he often wrote careless.
      C. It was generally doubted whether the women would permit the use of her apart-ment for intelligence operations.
      D. The probationer acts differently every time the officer visits him.
      E. Each of the newly appointed officers has 12 years of service.

25.   A. The North is the most industrialized region in the country.   25._____
      B. L. Patrick Gray 3d, the bureau's acting director, stated that, while "rehabilitation is fine" for some convicted criminals, "it is a useless gesture for those who resist every such effort."
      C. Careless driving, faulty mechanism, narrow or badly kept roads all play their part in causing accidents.
      D. The childrens' books were left in the bus.
      E. It was a matter of internal security; consequently, he felt no inclination to rescind his previous order.

KEY (CORRECT ANSWERS)

1.	C	11.	C
2.	B	12.	D
3.	D	13.	B
4.	C	14.	D
5.	E	15.	A
6.	A	16.	C
7.	C	17.	E
8.	B	18.	D
9.	B	19.	A
10.	C	20.	C

21.	B
22.	E
23.	B
24.	B
25.	D

TEST 2

DIRECTIONS: Each question or incomplete statement is followed by several suggested answers or completions. Select the one that BEST answers the question or completes the statement. *PRINT THE LETTER OF THE CORRECT ANSWER IN THE SPACE AT THE RIGHT.*

Questions 1-6.

DIRECTIONS: Each of Questions 1 through 6 consists of a statement which contains a word (one of those underlined) that is either incorrectly used because it is not in keeping with the meaning the quotation is evidently intended to convey, or is misspelled. There is only one INCORRECT word in each quotation. Of the four underlined words, determine if the first one should be replaced by the word lettered A, the second replaced by the word lettered B, the third replaced by the word lettered C, or the fourth replaced by the word lettered D. *PRINT THE LETTER OF THE REPLACEMENT WORD YOU HAVE SELECTED IN THE SPACE AT THE RIGHT.*

1. Whether one depends on <u>fluorescent</u> or artificial light or both, adequate <u>standards</u> should be <u>maintained</u> by means of <u>systematic</u> tests.   1.____

    A. natural   B. safeguards
    C. established   D. routine

2. A <u>police officer</u> has to be <u>prepared</u> to assume his <u>knowledge</u> as a social <u>scientist</u> in   2.____
    the <u>community</u>.

    A. forced   B. role
    C. philosopher   D. street

3. It is <u>practically</u> impossible to <u>indicate</u> whether a sentence is <u>too</u> long simply by <u>measuring</u>   3.____
    its length.

    A. almost   B. tell   C. very   D. guessing

4. Strong <u>leaders</u> are <u>required</u> to organize a community for delinquency prevention and for   4.____
    <u>dissemination</u> of organized <u>crime</u> and drug addiction.

    A. tactics   B. important   C. control   D. meetings

5. The <u>demonstrators</u> who were taken to the Criminal Courts building in <u>Manhattan</u>   5.____
    (because it was large enough to <u>accommodate</u> them), contended that the arrests were
    <u>unwarrented.</u>

    A. demonstraters   B. Manhatten
    C. accomodate   D. unwarranted

6. They were <u>guaranteed</u> a calm <u>atmosphere</u>, free from <u>harrassment</u>, which would be con-   6. ___
    ducive to quiet consideration of the <u>indictments</u>.

    A. guarenteed   B. atmospher
    C. harassment   D. inditements

Questions 7-11.

DIRECTIONS: Each of Questions 7 through 11 consists of a statement containing four words in capital letters. One of these words in capital letters is not in keeping with the meaning which the statement is evidently intended to carry. The four words in capital letters in each statement are reprinted after the statement. Print the capital letter preceding the one of the four words which does MOST to spoil the true meaning of the statement in the space at the right.

7. Retirement and pension systems are essential not only to provide employees with a means of support in the future, but also to prevent longevity and CHARITABLE consider- ations from UPSETTING the PROMOTIONAL opportunities for RETIRED members of the career service.

    A. charitable   B. upsetting
    C. promotional   D. retired

7.____

8. Within each major DIVISION in a properly set up public or private organization, provision is made so that each NECESSARY activity is CARED for and lines of authority and responsibility are clear-cut and INFINITE.

    A. division   B. necessary   C. cared   D. infinite

8.____

9. In public service, the scale of salaries paid must be INCIDENTAL to the services ren- dered, with due CONSIDERATION for the attraction of the desired MANPOWER and for the maintenance of a standard of living COMMENSURATE with the work to be per- formed.

    A. incidental   B. consideration
    C. manpower   D. commensurate

9.____

10. An understanding of the AIMS of an organization by the staff will AID greatly in increas- ing the DEMAND of the correspondence work of the office, and will to a large extent DETERMINE the nature of the correspondence.

    A. aims   B. aid   C. demand   D. determine

10.____

11. BECAUSE the Civil Service Commission strongly feels that the MERIT system is a key factor in the MAINTENANCE of democratic government, it has adopted as one of its major DEFENSES the progressive democratization of its own procedures in dealing with candidates for positions in the public service.

    A. Because   B. merit
    C. maintenance   D. defenses

11.____

Questions 12-14.

DIRECTIONS: Questions 12 through 14 consist of one sentence each. Each sentence con- tains an incorrectly used word. First, decide which is the incorrectly used word. Then, from among the options given, decide which word, when substituted for the incorrectly used word, makes the meaning of the sentence clear.

EXAMPLE:
The U.S. national income exhibits a pattern of long term deflection.
  A. reflection   B. subjection
  C. rejoicing   D. growth

The word *deflection* in the sentence does not convey the meaning the sentence evidently intended to convey. The word *growth* (Answer D), when substituted for the word *deflection,* makes the meaning of the sentence clear. Accordingly, the answer to the question is D.

12. The study commissioned by the joint committee fell compassionately short of the mark   12.____
and would have to be redone.

  A. successfully   B. insignificantly
  C. experimentally   D. woefully

13. He will not idly exploit any violation of the provisions of the order.   13.____

  A. tolerate   B. refuse   C. construe   D. guard

14. The defendant refused to be virile and bitterly protested service.   14.____

  A. irked   B. feasible   C. docile   D. credible

Questions 15-25.

DIRECTIONS: Questions 15 through 25 consist of short paragraphs. Each paragraph contains one word which is INCORRECTLY used because it is NOT in keeping with the meaning of the paragraph. Find the word in each paragraph which is INCORRECTLY used and then select as the answer the suggested word which should be substituted for the incorrectly used word.

SAMPLE QUESTION:
In determining who is to do the work in your unit, you will have to decide just who does what from day to day. One of your lowest responsibilities is to assign work so that everybody gets a fair share and that everyone can do his part well.
  A. new   B. old   C. important   D. performance

EXPLANATION:
The word which is NOT in keeping with the meaning of the paragraph is *lowest*. This is the INCORRECTLY used word. The suggested word *important* would be in keeping with the meaning of the paragraph and should be substituted for *lowest*. Therefore, the CORRECT answer is choice C.

15. If really good practice in the elimination of preventable injuries is to be achieved and held   15.____
in any establishment, top management must refuse full and definite responsibility and must apply a good share of its attention to the task.

  A. accept   B. avoidable   C. duties   D. problem

16. Recording the human face for identification is by no means the only service performed by   16.____
the camera in the field of investigation. When the trial of any issue takes place, a word picture is sought to be distorted to the court of incidents, occurrences, or events which are in dispute.

A.   appeals
C.   portrayed

B.   description
D.   deranged

17. In the collection of physical evidence, it cannot be emphasized too strongly that a haphazard systematic search at the scene of the crime is vital. Nothing must be overlooked.
Often the only leads in a case will come from the results of this search.

17.____

A.   important
C.   proof

B.   investigation
D.   thorough

18. If an investigator has reason to suspect that the witness is mentally stable, or a habitual
drunkard, he should leave no stone unturned in his investigation to determine if the witness was under the influence of liquor or drugs, or was mentally unbalanced either at the
time of the occurrence to which he testified or at the time of the trial.

18.____

A.   accused   B.   clue   C.   deranged   D.   question

19. The use of records is a valuable step in crime investigation and is the main reason every
department should maintain accurate reports. Crimes are not committed through the use
of departmental records alone but from the use of all records, of almost every type, wherever they may be found and whenever they give any incidental information regarding the
criminal.

19.____

A.   accidental
C.   reported

B.   necessary
D.   solved

20. In the years since passage of the Harrison Narcotic Act of 1914, making the possession
of opium amphetamines illegal in most circumstances, drug use has become a subject of
considerable scientific interest and investigation. There is at present a voluminous litera-
ture on drug use of various kinds.

20.____

A.   ingestion
C.   addiction

B.   derivatives
D.   opiates

21. Of course, the fact that criminal laws are extremely patterned in definition does not mean
that the majority of persons who violate them are dealt with as criminals. Quite the contrary, for a great many forbidden acts are voluntarily engaged in within situations of pri-
vacy and go unobserved and unreported.

21.____

A.   symbolic
C.   scientific

B.   casual
D.   broad-gauged

22. The most punitive way to study punishment is to focus attention on the pattern of punitive
action: to study how a penalty is applied, to study what is done to or taken from an
offender.

22.____

A.   characteristic
C.   objective

B.   degrading
D.   distinguished

23. The most common forms of punishment in times past have been death, physical torture,
mutilation, branding, public humiliation, fines, forfeits of property, banishment, transportation, and imprisonment. Although this list is by no means differentiated, practically every
form of punishment has had several variations and applications.

23.____

A.   specific
C.   exhaustive

B.   simple
D.   characteristic

24. There is another important line of inference between ordinary and professional criminals, and that is the source from which they are recruited. The professional criminal seems to be drawn from legitimate employment and, in many instances, from parallel vocations or pursuits.

24.____

   A. demarcation   B. justification
   C. superiority   D. reference

25. He took the position that the success of the program was insidious on getting additional revenue.

25.____

   A. reputed   B. contingent
   C. failure   D. indeterminate

KEY (CORRECT ANSWERS)

1.	A	11.	D
2.	B	12.	D
3.	B	13.	A
4.	C	14.	C
5.	D	15.	A
6.	C	16.	C
7.	D	17.	D
8.	D	18.	C
9.	A	19.	D
10.	C	20.	B

21. D
22. C
23. C
24. A
25. B

TEST 3

DIRECTIONS: Each question or incomplete statement is followed by several suggested answers or completions. Select the one that BEST answers the question or completes the statement. *PRINT THE LETTER OF THE CORRECT ANSWER IN THE SPACE AT THE RIGHT.*

Questions 1-5.

DIRECTIONS: Question 1 through 5 are to be answered on the basis of the following:

You are a supervising officer in an investigative unit. Earlier in the day, you directed Detectives Tom Dixon and Sal Mayo to investigate a reported assault and robbery in a liquor store within your area of jurisdiction.

Detective Dixon has submitted to you a preliminary investigative report containing the following information:

- At 1630 hours on 2/20, arrived at Joe's Liquor Store at 350 SW Avenue with Detective Mayo to investigate A & R.
- At store interviewed Rob Ladd, store manager, who stated that he and Joe Brown (store owner) had been stuck up about ten minutes prior to our arrival.
- Ladd described the robbers as male whites in their late teens or early twenties. Further stated that one of the robbers displayed what appeared to be an automatic pistol as he entered the store, and said, *Give us the money or we'll kill you.* Ladd stated that Brown then reached under the counter where he kept a loaded .38 caliber pistol. Several shots followed, and Ladd threw himself to the floor.
- The robbers fled, and Ladd didn't know if any money had been taken.
- At this point, Ladd realized that Brown was unconscious on the floor and bleeding from a head wound.
- Ambulance called by Ladd, and Brown was removed by same to General Hospital.
- Personally interviewed John White, 382 Dartmouth Place, who stated he was inside store at the time of occurrence. White states that he hid behind a wine display upon hearing someone say, *Give us the money.* He then heard shots and saw two young men run from the store to a yellow car parked at the curb. White was unable to further describe auto. States the taller of the two men drove the car away while the other sat on passenger side in front.
- Recovered three spent .38 caliber bullets from premises and delivered them to Crime Lab.
- To General Hospital at 1800 hours but unable to interview Brown, who was under sedation and suffering from shock and a laceration of the head.
- Alarm #12487 transmitted for car and occupants.
- Case Active.

Based solely on the contents of the preliminary investigation submitted by Detective Dixon, select one sentence from the following groups of sentences which is MOST accurate and is grammatically correct.

1.   A. Both robbers were armed.   1._____
     B. Each of the robbers were described as a male white.
     C. Neither robber was armed.
     D. Mr. Ladd stated that one of the robbers was armed.

2.   A. Mr. Brown fired three shots from his revolver.   2._____
     B. Mr. Brown was shot in the head by one of the robbers.
     C. Mr. Brown suffered a gunshot wound of the head during the course of the robbery.
     D. Mr. Brown was taken to General Hospital by ambulance.

3.   A. Shots were fired after one of the robbers said, *Give us* the money or we'll kill you.   3._____
     B. After one of the robbers demanded the money from Mr. Brown, he fired a shot.
     C. The preliminary investigation Indicated that although Mr. Brown did not have a license for the gun, he was justified in using deadly physical force.
     D. Mr. Brown was interviewed at General Hospital.

4.   A. Each of the witnesses were customers in the store at the time of occurrence.   4._____
     B. Neither of the witnesses interviewed was the owner of the liquor store.
     C. Neither of the witnesses interviewed were the owner of the store.
     D. Neither of the witnesses was employed by Mr. Brown.

5.   A. Mr. Brown arrived at General Hospital at about 5:00 P.M.   5._____
     B. Neither of the robbers was injured during the robbery.
     C. The robbery occurred at 3:30 P.M. on February 10.
     D. One of the witnesses called the ambulance.

Questions 6-10.

DIRECTIONS: Each of Questions 6 through 10 consists of information given in outline form and four sentences labelled A, B, C, and D. For each question, choose the one sentence which CORRECTLY expresses the information given in outline form and which also displays PROPER English usage.

6. Client's Name - Joanna Jones   6._____
   Number of Children - 3
   Client's Income - None
   Client's Marital Status - Single

     A. Joanna Jones is an unmarried client with three children who have no income.
     B. Joanna Jones, who is single and has no income, a client she has three children.
     C. Joanna Jones, whose three children are clients, is single and has no income.
     D. Joanna Jones, who has three children, is an unmarried client with no income.

7. Client's Name - Bertha Smith   7._____
   Number of Children - 2
   Client's Rent - $105 per month
   Number of Rooms - 4

A. Bertha Smith, a client, pays $105 per month for her four rooms with two children.
B. Client Bertha Smith has two children and pays $105 per month for four rooms.
C. Client Bertha Smith is paying $105 per month for two children with four rooms.
D. For four rooms and two children client Bertha Smith pays $105 per month.

8. Name of Employee - Cynthia Dawes
Number of Cases Assigned - 9
Date Cases were Assigned - 12/16
Number of Assigned Cases Completed - 8

8.____

A. On December 16, employee Cynthia Dawes was assigned nine cases; she has completed eight of these cases.
B. Cynthia Dawes, employee on December 16, assigned nine cases, completed eight.
C. Being employed on December 16, Cynthia Dawes completed eight of nine assigned cases.
D. Employee Cynthia Dawes, she was assigned nine cases and completed eight, on December 16.

9. Place of Audit - Broadway Center
Names of Auditors - Paul Cahn, Raymond Perez
Date of Audit - 11/20
Number of Cases Audited - 41

9.____

A. On November 20, at the Broadway Center 41 cases was audited by auditors Paul Cahn and Raymond Perez.
B. Auditors Raymond Perez and Paul Cahn has audited 41 cases at the Broadway Center on November 20.
C. At the Broadway Center, on November 20, auditors Paul Cahn and Raymond Perez audited 41 cases.
D. Auditors Paul Cahn and Raymond Perez at the Broadway Center, on November 20, is auditing 41 cases.

10. Name of Client - Barbra Levine
Client's Monthly Income - $210
Client's Monthly Expenses - $452

10.____

A. Barbra Levine is a client, her monthly income is $210 and her monthly expenses is $452.
B. Barbra Levine's monthly income is $210 and she is a client, with whose monthly expenses are $452.
C. Barbra Levine is a client whose monthly income is $210 and whose monthly expenses are $452.
D. Barbra Levine, a client, is with a monthly income which is $210 and monthly expenses which are $452.

Questions 11-13.

DIRECTIONS: Questions 11 through 13 involve several statements of fact presented in a very simple way. These statements of fact are followed by 4 choices which attempt to incorporate all of the facts into one logical sentence which is properly constructed and grammatically correct.

11.   I.   Mr. Brown was sweeping the sidewalk in front of his house.   11.____
       II.   He was sweeping it because it was dirty.
      III. He swept the refuse into the street
      IV. Police Officer Green gave him a ticket.

Which one of the following BEST presents the information given above?

    A.   Because his sidewalk was dirty, Mr. Brown received a ticket from Officer Green when he swept the refuse into the street.
    B.   Police Officer Green gave Mr. Brown a ticket because his sidewalk was dirty and he swept the refuse into the street.
    C.   Police Officer Green gave Mr. Brown a ticket for sweeping refuse into the street because his sidewalk was dirty.
    D.   Mr. Brown, who was sweeping refuse from his dirty sidewalk into the street, was given a ticket by Police Officer Green.

12.   I.   Sergeant Smith radioed for help.   12.____
       II.   The sergeant did so because the crowd was getting larger.
      III. It was 10:00 A.M. when he made his call.
      IV. Sergeant Smith was not in uniform at the time of occurrence.

Which one of the following BEST presents the information given above?

    A.   Sergeant Smith, although not on duty at the time, radioed for help at 10 o'clock because the crowd was getting uglier.
    B.   Although not in uniform, Sergeant Smith called for help at 10:00 A.M. because the crowd was getting uglier.
    C.   Sergeant Smith radioed for help at 10:00 A.M. because the crowd was getting larger.
    D.   Although he was not in uniform, Sergeant Smith radioed for help at 10:00 A.M. because the crowd was getting larger.

13.   I.   The payroll office is open on Fridays.   13.____
       II.   Paychecks are distributed from 9:00 A.M. to 12 Noon.
      III. The office is open on Fridays because that's the only day the payroll staff is available.
      IV. It is open for the specified hours in order to permit employees to cash checks at the bank during lunch hour.

The choice below which MOST clearly and accurately presents the above idea is:

    A.   Because the payroll office is open on Fridays from 9:00 A.M. to 12 Noon, employees can cash their checks when the payroll staff is available.
    B.   Because the payroll staff is only available on Fridays until noon, employees can cash their checks during their lunch hour.
    C.   Because the payroll staff is available only on Fridays, the office is open from 9:00 A.M. to 12 Noon to allow employees to cash their checks.
    D.   Because of payroll staff availability, the payroll office is open on Fridays. It is open from 9:00 A.M. to 12 Noon so that distributed paychecks can be cashed at the bank while employees are on their lunch hour.

Questions 14-16.

DIRECTIONS: In each of Questions 14 through 16, the four sentences are from a paragraph in a report. They are not in the right order. Which of the following arrangements is the BEST one?

14. I.   An executive may answer a letter by writing his reply on the face of the letter itself instead of having a return letter typed.
     II. This procedure is efficient because it saves the executive's time, the typist's time, and saves office file space.
     III. Copying machines are used in small offices as well as large offices to save time and money in making brief replies to business letters.
     IV. A copy is made on a copying machine to go into the company files, while the original is mailed back to the sender.
     The CORRECT answer is:

     A. I, II, IV, III   B. I, IV, II, III
     C. III, I, IV, II   D. III, IV, II, I

15. I.   Most organizations favor one of the types but always include the others to a lesser degree.
     II. However, we can detect a definite trend toward greater use of symbolic control.
     III. We suggest that our local police agencies are today primarily utilizing material control.
     IV. Control can be classified into three types: physical, material, and symbolic.
     The CORRECT answer is:

     A. IV, II, III, I   B. II, I, IV, III
     C. III, IV, II, I   D. IV, I, III, II

16. I.   They can and do take advantage of ancient political and geographical boundaries, which often give them sanctuary from effective police activity.
     II. This country is essentially a country of small police forces, each operating independently within the limits of its jurisdiction.
     III. The boundaries that define and limit police operations do not hinder the movement of criminals, of course.
     IV. The machinery of law enforcement in America is fragmented, complicated, and frequently overlapping.
     The CORRECT answer is:

     A. III, I, II, IV   B. II, IV, I, III
     C. IV, II, III, I   D. IV, III, II, I

17. Examine the following sentence, and then choose from below the words which should be inserted in the blank spaces to produce the best sentence.
     The unit has exceeded _____ goals and the employees are satisfied with _____ accomplishments.

     A. their, it's   B. it's, it's
     C. its, there   D. its, their

18. Examine the following sentence, and then choose from below the words which should be   18.____
inserted in the blank spaces to produce the best sentence.
Research indicates that employees who _____ no opportunity for close social relationships often find their work unsatisfying, and this _____ of satisfaction often
reflects itself in low production.

    A. have, lack   B. have, excess
    C. has, lack   D. has, excess

19. Words in a sentence must be arranged properly to make sure that the intended meaning   19.____
of the sentence is clear. The sentence below that does NOT make sense because a
clause has been separated from the word on which its meaning depends is:

    A. To be a good writer, clarity is necessary.
    B. To be a good writer, you must write clearly.
    C. You must write clearly to be a good writer.
    D. Clarity is necessary to good writing.

Questions 20-21.

DIRECTIONS: Each of Questions 20 and 21 consists of a statement which contains a word
(one of those underlined) that is either incorrectly used because it is not in
keeping with the meaning the quotation is evidently intended to convey, or is
misspelled. There is only one INCORRECT word in each quotation. Of the four
underlined words, determine if the first one should be replaced by the word lettered A, the second one replaced by the word lettered B, the third one
replaced by the word lettered C, or the fourth one replaced by the word lettered D. *PRINT THE LETTER OF THE REPLACEMENT WORD YOU HAVE
SELECTED IN THE SPACE AT THE RIGHT.*

20. The <u>alleged</u> killer was <u>occasionally</u> <u>permitted</u> to <u>excercise</u> in the corridor.   20.____

    A. alledged   B. ocasionally
    C. permited   D. exercise

21. Defense <u>counsel</u> stated, in <u>affect</u>, that <u>their</u> conduct was <u>permissible</u> under the First   21.____
Amendment.

    A. council   B. effect
    C. there   D. permissable

Question 22.

DIRECTIONS: Question 22 consists of one sentence. This sentence contains an incorrectly
used word. First, decide which is the incorrectly used word. Then, from among
the options given, decide which word, when substituted for the incorrectly used
word, makes the meaning of the sentence clear.

22. As today's violence has no single cause, so its causes have no single scheme.   22.____

    A. deference   B. cure   C. flaw   D. relevance

23. In the sentence, *A man in a light-grey suit waited thirty-five minutes in the ante-room for the all-important document,* the word IMPROPERLY hyphenated is

    A. light-grey   B. thirty-five
    C. ante-room   D. all-important

23.____

24. In the sentence, *The candidate wants to file his application for preference before it is too late,* the word *before* is used as a(n)

    A. preposition   B. subordinating conjunction
    C. pronoun   D. adverb

24.____

25. In the sentence, *The perpetrators ran from the scene,* the word *from* is a

    A. preposition   B. pronoun
    C. verb   D. conjunction

25.____

KEY (CORRECT ANSWERS)

1.	D		11.	D
2.	D		12.	D
3.	A		13.	D
4.	B		14.	C
5.	D		15.	D
6.	D		16.	C
7.	B		17.	D
8.	A		18.	A
9.	C		19.	A
10.	C		20.	D

21.	B
22.	B
23.	C
24.	B
25.	A

REPORT WRITING

EXAMINATION SECTION
TEST 1

DIRECTIONS: Each question or incomplete statement is followed by several suggested answers or completions. Select the one that BEST answers the question or completes the statement. *PRINT THE LETTER OF THE CORRECT ANSWER IN THE SPACE AT THE RIGHT.*

Questions 1-5.

DIRECTIONS: Questions 1 through 5 are to be answered on the basis of the Report of Offense that appears below.

REPORT OF OFFENSE   Report No. *26743*
                                         Date of Report *10-12*

Inmate *Joseph Brown*
Age *27*   Number *61274*
Sentence *90 days*   Assignment *KU-187*
Place of offense *R.P.W., 4-1*   Date of offense *10/11/*
Offense *Assaulting inmate*
Details *During 9:00 P.M., cellblock cleanup, inmate John Jones asked for pail being used by Brown. Brown refused. Correction officer requested that Brown comply. Brown then threw pail at Jones with intent to injure him and said he would "get" Jones. Jones not hurt.*

Force used by officer *None*
Name of reporting officer *R. Rodriguez*   No. *C-2056*
Name of superior officer *P. Ferguson*

---

1. The person who made out this report is   1.____

   A. Joseph Brown   B. John Jones
   C. R. Rodriguez   D. P. Ferguson

2. Disregarding the details, the specific offense reported was   2.____

   A. insulting a fellow inmate
   B. assaulting a fellow inmate
   C. injuring a fellow inmate
   D. disobeying a correction officer

3. The number of the inmate who committed the offense is   3.____

   A. 26743   B. 61274   C. KU-187   D. C-2056

4. The offense took place on   4.____

   A. October 11   B. June 12
   C. December 10   D. November 13

5. The place where the offense occurred is identified in the report as 5.____

    A. Brown's cell   B. Jones' cell
    C. KU-187   D. R.P.W., 4-1

Questions 6-10.

DIRECTIONS: Questions 6 through 10 are to be answered on the basis of the Report of Loss or Theft that appears below.

REPORT OF LOSS OR THEFT   Date: *12/4*   Time: *9:15 A.M.*

Complaint made by: *Richard Aldridge*   ☐ Owner
                      306 S. Walter St.   ☒ Other - explain:
                                           Head of Acctg. Dept.

Type of property: *Computer*   Value: *$'450.00*
Description: *Dell Inspiron laptop*
Location: *768 N. Margin Ave., Accounting Dept., 3rd Floor*
Time: *Overnight 12/3 - 12/4*
Circumstances: *Mr. Aldridge reports he arrived at work 8:45 A.M., found office door open and machine missing. Nothing else reported missing. I investigated and found signs of forced entry; door lock was broken.*
                 Signature of Reporting Officer: *B.L. Ramirez*

Notify:
   ☐ Q Building & Grounds Office, 768 N. Margin Ave.
   ☐ Q Lost Property Office, 110 Brand Ave. 0
   ☒ Security Office, 703 N. Wide Street

---

6. The person who made this complaint is 6.____

    A. a secretary   B. a security officer
    C. Richard Aldridge   D. B.L. Ramirez

7. The report concerns a computer that has been 7.____

    A. lost   B. damaged   C. stolen   D. sold

8. The person who took the computer PROBABLY entered the office through 8.____

    A. a door   B. a window
    C. the roof   D. the basement

9. When did the head of the Accounting Department FIRST notice that the computer was missing? 9.____

    A. December 4 at 9:15 A.M.
    B. December 4 at 8:45 A.M.
    C. The night of December 3
    D. The night of December 4

10. The event described in the report took place at   10.____

    A. 306 South Walter Street   B. 768 North Margin Avenue
    C. 110 Brand Avenue   D. 703 North Wide Street

Questions 11-15.

DIRECTIONS: Questions 11 through 15 are to be answered on the basis of the following excerpt from a recorded Annual Report of the Police Department. This material should be read first and then referred to in answering these questions, which are to be answered SOLELY on the basis of the material herein contained.

LEGAL BUREAU

One of the more important functions of this bureau is to analyze and furnish the department with pertinent information concerning Federal and State statutes and local laws which affect the department, law enforcement or crime prevention. In addition, all measures introduced in the State Legislature and the City Council, which may affect this department, are carefully reviewed by members of the Legal Bureau and, where necessary, opinions and recommendations thereon are prepared.

Another important function of this office is the prosecution of cases in the Magistrate's Courts. This is accomplished by assignment of attorneys who are members of the Legal Bureau to appear in those cases which are deemed to raise issues of importance to the department or questions of law which require technical presentation to facilitate proper determination; and also in those cases where request is made for such appearance by a magistrate, some other official of the city, or a member of the force. Attorneys are regularly assigned to prosecute all cases in the Family Court.

Proposed legislation was prepared and sponsored for introduction in the State Legislature and, at this writing, one of these proposals has already been enacted into law and five others are presently on the Governor's desk awaiting executive action. The new law prohibits the sale or possession of a hypodermic syringe or needle by an unauthorized person. The bureau's proposals awaiting executive action pertain to: an amendment to the Code of Criminal Procedure prohibiting desk officers from taking bail in gambling cases or in cases mentioned in Section 552, Code of Criminal Procedure, including confidence men and swindlers as jostlers in the Penal Law; prohibiting the sale of switch-blade knives of any size to children under 16 and bills extending the licensing period of gunsmiths.

The Legal Bureau has regularly cooperated with the Corporation Counsel and the District Attorneys in respect to matters affecting this department, and has continued to advise and represent the Police Athletic League, the Police Sports Association, the Police Relief Fund, and the Police Pension Fund.

The following is a statistical report of the activities of the bureau during the current year as compared with the previous year:

	Current Year	Previous Year
Memoranda of law prepared	68	83
Legal matters forwarded to Corporation Counsel	122	144
Letters requesting legal information	756	807
Letters requesting departmental records	139	111
Matters for publication	17	26
Court appearances of members of bureau	4,678	4,621
Conferences	94	103
Lectures at Police Academy	30	33
Reports on proposed legislation	194	255
Deciphering of codes	79	27
Expert testimony	31	16
Notices to court witnesses	55	81
Briefs prepared	22	18
Court papers prepared	258	---

11. One of the functions of the Legal Bureau is to 11._____

    A. review and make recommendations on proposed federal laws affecting law enforcement
    B. prepare opinions on all measures introduced in the state legislature and the City Council
    C. furnish the Police Department with pertinent information concerning all new federal and state laws
    D. analyze all laws affecting the work of the Police Department

12. The Legal Bureau sponsored a bill that would 12._____

    A. extend the licenses of gunsmiths
    B. prohibit the sale of switch-blade knives to children of any size
    C. place confidence men and swindlers in the same category as jostlers in the Penal Law
    D. prohibit desk officers from admitting gamblers, confidence men, and swindlers to bail

13. From the report, it is NOT reasonable to infer that 13._____

    A. fewer bills affecting the Police Department were introduced in the current year
    B. the preparation of court papers was a new activity assumed in the current year
    C. the Code of Criminal Procedure authorizes desk officers to accept bail in certain cases
    D. the penalty for jostling and swindling is the same

14. According to the statistical report, the activity showing the GREATEST percentage of decrease in the current year compared with the previous year was 14._____

    A. matters for publication
    B. reports on proposed legislation
    C. notices to court witnesses
    D. memoranda of law prepared

15. According to the report, the percentage of bills prepared and sponsored by the Legal Bureau, which were passed by the State Legislature and sent to the Governor for approval, was

    A. approximately 3.1%
    B. approximately 2.6%
    C. approximately .5%
    D. not capable of determination from the data given

15._____

———

KEY (CORRECT ANSWERS)

1. C	6. C
2. B	7. C
3. B	8. A
4. A	9. B
5. D	10. B

11. D
12. C
13. D
14. A
15. D

———

TEST 2

DIRECTIONS: Each question or incomplete statement is followed by several suggested answers or completions. Select the one that BEST answers the question or completes the statement. *PRINT THE LETTER OF THE CORRECT ANSWER IN THE SPACE AT THE RIGHT.*

Questions 1-2.

DIRECTIONS: Questions 1 and 2 are to be answered on the basis of the Instructions, the Bridge and Tunnel Officer's Toll Report form, and the situation given below. The questions ask how the report form should be filled in based on the Instructions and the information given in the situation.

INSTRUCTIONS

Assume that a Bridge and Tunnel Officer on duty in a toll booth must make an entry on the following report form immediately after each incident in which a vehicle driver does not pay the correct toll.

```
┌─────────────────────────────────────────────────────────────────────┐
│            BRIDGE AND TUNNEL OFFICER'S TOLL REPORT                     │
│                                                                       │
│   Officer _____        Date _____          │
│                                                                       │
│              Type of        Toll                                      │
│       Time   Vehicle     Collected      Explanation of Entry          │
│                                                                       │
│   1. ____    _____    _____      _____              │
│   2. ____    _____    _____      _____              │
│                                                                       │
│      ____    _____    _____      _____              │
└─────────────────────────────────────────────────────────────────────┘
```

SITUATION

John McDonald is a Bridge and Tunnel Officer assigned to toll booth 4, between the hours of 11 P.M. and 1 A.M. On this particular tour, two incidents occurred. At 11:43 P.M., a five-axle truck stopped at the toll booth and Officer McDonald collected a $2.50 toll from the driver. As the truck passed, he realized the toll should have been $3.30, and he quickly copied the vehicle's license plate number as M724HJ. At 12:34 A.M., a motorcycle went through toll lane 4 without paying the toll. The motorcycle did not have any license plate.

1. The entry which should be made on line 1 in the second column is   1.___

   A. 11:43 P.M.   B. 12:34 A.M.
   C. five-axle truck   D. motorcycle

2. The above passage does NOT provide the information necessary to fill in which of the   2.___
   following items?

   A. Officer   B. Date
   C. Line 1, Toll Collected   D. Line 2, Time

Questions 3-7.

DIRECTIONS: Questions 3 through 7 are to be answered on the basis of the Fact Situation and the Report of Inmate Injury form below. The questions ask how the report form should be filled in, based on the information given in the Fact Situation.

FACT SITUATION

Peter Miller is a Correction Officer assigned to duty in Cell-block A. His superior officer is John Doakes. Miller was on duty at 1:30 P.M. on March 21 when he heard a scream for help from Cell 12. He hurried to Cell 12 and found inmate Richard Rogers stamping out a flaming book of matches. Inmate John Jones was screaming. It seems that Jones had accidentally set fire to the entire book of matches while lighting a cigarette, and he had burned his left hand. Smoking was permitted at this hour. Miller reported the incident by phone, and Jones was escorted to the dispensary where his hand was treated at 2:00 P.M. by Dr. Albert Lorillo. Dr. Lorillo determined that Jones could return to his cellblock, but that he should be released from work for four days. The doctor scheduled a re-examination for March 22. A routine investigation of the incident was made by James Lopez. Jones confirmed to this officer that the above statement of the situation was correct.

REPORT OF INMATE INJURY

(1) Name of inmate _____ (2) Assignment _____
(3) Number _____ (4) Location _____
(5) Nature of injury _____ (6) Date _____
(7) Details (how, when, where injury was incurred) _____
_____
(8) Received medical attention: date _____ time _____
(9) Treatment _____
(10) Disposition (check one or more):
___(10-1) Return to housing area ___(10-2) Return to duty
___(10-3) Work release ___ days ___(10-4) Re-examine in ___ days
(11) Employee reporting injury _____
(12) Employee's supervisor or superior officer _____
(13) Medical officer treating injury _____
(14) Investigating officer _____
(15) Head of institution _____

---

3. Which of the following should be entered in Item 1?   3.____

   A. Peter Miller   B. John Doakes
   C. Richard Rogers   D. John Jones

4. Which of the following should be entered in Item 11?   4.____

   A. Peter Miller   B. James Lopez
   C. Richard Rogers   D. John Jones

5. Which of the following should be entered in Item 8?   5.____

   A. 2/21, 1:30 P.M.   B. 2/21, 2:00 P.M.
   C. 3/21, 1:30 P.M.   D. 3/21, 2:00 P.M.

6. For Item 10, which of the following should be checked?   6.____

    A. 10-4 *only*   B. 10-1 and 10-4
    C. 10-1, 10-3, and 10-4   D. 10-2, 10-3, and 10-4

7. Of the following items, which one CANNOT be filled in on the basis of the information   7.____
   given in the Fact Situation? Item

    A. 12   B. 13   C. 14   D. 15

Questions 8-11.

DIRECTIONS: Questions 8 through 11 are to be answered on the basis of the Fact Situation
and the Traffic Control Report form below. Read the Fact Situation carefully,
and examine the blank report form. The questions ask how the report form
should be filled in based on the information given in the Fact Situation.

FACT SITUATION

Mary Fields is a Traffic Control Agent. Her City Employee Number is Z90019. She is
assigned to duty at the intersection of Silver Street and Amber Avenue. On the morning of
May 15, she arrives at this intersection at 8:00 A.M. and sees that there is a new *patch job* on
the surface of Amber Avenue in the middle of the pedestrian crosswalk and near the north-
west corner of the intersection. The day before, an emergency crew was digging here. The
hole is now closed and resurfaced, but the patch job on the surface was not done very well.
The patch is nearly an inch higher than the surrounding surface, and it has a sharp edge that
pedestrians are likely to trip on. Mary Fields thinks this condition is dangerous, and she
reports it on the Traffic Control Report form.

TRAFFIC CONTROL REPORT:
DEFECTIVE EQUIPMENT OR UNSAFE CONDITION

1. Date of observation _____   2. Time _____
3. Exact location _____
4. Type of equipment or condition found to be defective or
    unsafe _____
5. Type of defect _____
6. Name of reporting Agent_____
7. Employee no. _____   8. Precinct no._____

---

8. Which of the following should be entered in Blank 3?   8.____

    A. Silver Street at Amber Avenue, near northeast corner
    B. Silver Street at Amber Avenue, near northwest corner
    C. Amber Avenue at Silver Street, near northeast corner
    D. Amber Avenue at Silver Street, near northwest corner

9. Which of the following should be entered in Blank 4?   9.____

    A. Pedestrian traffic signals
    B. Pedestrian crosswalk markings
    C. Surface patch
    D. Unsafe condition

10. The information called for in Blank 5 is needed to determine what kind of repairs must be   10.____
made and what kind of repair crew must be sent.
Which of the following entries for Blank 5 will be MOST useful to the people who
receive this report in deciding what kind of repair crew to assign to the job?

    A.   Pedestrians may stumble and fall.
    B.   New patch is higher than rest of surface.
    C.   Emergency crew dug a hole here.
    D.   Street repairs were not done very well.

11. There is one blank on the form for which the Fact Situation does not provide the informa-   11.____
tion needed.
The blank that CANNOT be filled out on the basis of the information given is Blank

    A. 2   B. 6   C. 7   D. 8

Questions 12-15.

DIRECTIONS: Questions 12 through 15 are to be answered on the basis of the Fact Situation
and the Report of Arrest form below. Questions ask how the report form
should be filled in based on the information given in the Fact Situation.

FACT SITUATION

Jesse Stein is a special officer (security officer) who is assigned to a welfare center at
435 East Smythe Street, Brooklyn. He was on duty there Thursday morning, February 1. At
10:30 A.M., a client named Jo Ann Jones, 40 years old, arrived with her 10-year-old son
Peter. Another client, Mary Alice Wiell, 45 years old, immediately began to insult Mrs. Jones.
When Mrs. Jones told her to *go away,* Mrs. Wiell pulled out a long knife. The special officer
(security officer) intervened and requested Mrs. Wiell to drop the knife. She would not, and he
had to use necessary force to disarm her. He arrested her on charges of disorderly conduct,
harassment, and possession of a dangerous weapon. Mrs. Wiell lives at 118 Heally Street,
Brooklyn, Apartment 4F, and she is unemployed. The reason for her aggressive behavior is
not known.

```
┌─────────────────────────────────────────────────────────────────────────────┐
│ REPORT OF ARREST                                                              │
│                                                                               │
│ (01) _____     (08 _____     │
│      (Prisoner's surname) (first) (initial)        (Precinct)                 │
│                                                                               │
│ (02) _____     (09) _____     │
│      (Address)                                     (Date of arrest)           │
│                                                    (Month, Day)               │
│                                                                               │
│ (03) _____ (04) _____ (05) _____                                 │
│      (Date of birth)   (Age)        (Sex)    (10) _____      │
│                                                    (Time of arrest)           │
│                                                                               │
│ (06) _____ (07) _____      (11) _____      │
│      (Occupation)   (Where employed)               (Place of arrest)          │
│                                                                               │
│ (12) _____        │
│      (Specific offenses)                                                      │
│                                                                               │
│ (13) _____     (14) _____     │
│      (Arresting officer)                           (Officer's No.)            │
└─────────────────────────────────────────────────────────────────────────────┘
```

12. What entry should be made in Blank 01?   12.____

    A. Jo Ann Jones   B. Jones, Jo Ann
    C. Mary Wiell   D. Wiell, Mary A.

13. Which of the following should be entered in Blank 04?   13.____

    A. 40   B. 40's
    C. 45   D. Middle-aged

14. Which of the following should be entered in Blank 09?   14.____

    A. Wednesday, February 1, 10:30 A.M.
    B. February 1
    C. Thursday morning, February 2
    D. Morning, February 4

15. Of the following, which would be the BEST entry to make in Blank 11? 15.____

    A. Really Street Welfare Center
    B. Brooklyn
    C. 435 E. Smythe St., Brooklyn
    D. 118 Heally St., Apt. 4F

KEY (CORRECT ANSWERS)

1.	C	6.	C
2.	B	7.	D
3.	D	8.	D
4.	A	9.	C
5.	D	10.	B

11.	D
12.	D
13.	C
14.	B
15.	C

———